New Issues in Panchayati Raj

- Empowering Panchayats: Handbook for Master Trainers
- पंचायतों का सशक्तिकरण: प्रधान प्रशिक्षकों के लिए पुस्तिका

About the Rajiv Gandhi Foundation

The Rajiv Gandhi Foundation, established in 1991, is inspired by the vision of a nation that is modern, an economy that is strong and a society that is just. The Foundation is independent of party of political affiliation.

The Foundation works to provide enlarged opportunities to the underprivileged and the deprived. It supports projects in the field of literacy, woman and child development, natural resource management, science and technology and disabled persons' welfare.

Recalling Rajiv Gandhi's vision of a decentralised democracy, the Foundation established a Task Force on Panchayati Raj in 1993 to monitor the implementation of the 73rd Constitutional Amendment Act. The Task Force has been involved in country-wide advocacy and awareness building on the one hand, and developing training modules for panchayati raj functionaries on the other. This book is the eighteenth publication brought out by the Task Force.

About the Authors

D. Bandyopadhyay, IAS (Retd.) was the Secretary, Ministry of Rural Development and Secretary (Revenue), Ministry of Finance, Government of India; Executive Director, Asian Development Bank; and is presently connected in different senior capacities with various States and Cenral Organisations as also civil society organisations.

Dr. Amitava Mukherjee is the Executive Director of Development Tracks, New Delhi, a knowledge company and is currently Chief Technical Adviser (Pro-poor Public-Private Sector Partnership), with the United Nations, Economic and Social Council for Asia and the Pacific, Bangkok. He was earlier Professor of Economics and Planning, Lal Bahadur Shastri National Academy of Administration, Mussoorie and Consultant to various UN Agencies and International Organisations. He has written extensively on decentralisation, poverty and hunger, with over thirty books and numerous papers to his credit.

NEW ISSUES IN PANCHAYATI RAJ

D. BANDYOPADHYAY
AMITAVA MUKHERJEE

Published for
Task Force on Panchayati Raj
RAJIV GANDHI FOUNDATION
by
CONCEPT PUBLISHING COMPANY, NEW DELHI-110059

ISBN 81-8069-073-3

First Published 2004

Published and Printed by
Ashok Kumar Mittal
Concept Publishing Company,
A/15-16, Commercial Block, Mohan Garden,
New Delhi-110059 (INDIA)

Phones : 25351460, 25351794
Fax : 091-11-25357103
Email : publishing@conceptpub.com

Preface

This book is a valuable by-product of the Project entitled "Strengthening Panchayati Raj System—A Training Intervention" funded by the Ford Foundation. Towards the end of the Project, the Task Force wanted to assess the current situation in panchayats particularly relating to participation of women in the process of local governance. It became a common knowledge that attempts were being made to deviate from the main spirit of decentralisation of governance as mandated under the 73rd Constitutional Amendment. Not only parallel structures were being created in the name of efficient implementation of some projects, other institutional road-blocks were also being set up to ensure the dominance of the elite political establishment both at the State and the Central levels. MLAs and MPs wanted an effective executive role in the PRIs, often being oblivious of their roles as members of legislative bodies.

Setting up of Self-Help Groups, particularly, for women was an important step in ensuring participation by them in public matters. While these bodies could act as interest groups to espouse their cause through panchayats, particularly, at the village level, attempts were made in various States to bypass the panchayats and to give resources to them direct for various programmes. Somehow or the other it looked that the existing political establishments could not accept panchayats as a third stratum of governance in India and felt rather threatened because of the emergence of PRIs mandated by the Constitution.

Members of the Task Force and their friends/associates decided to record their experiences and views on various aspects of panchayats as it obtained around 2002. Contributors are well-known in their fields of activities and this friendly critique of the situation a decade after the Constitutional

Amendment is expected to help those who seriously consider the strengthening the base of our Republic by empowering the little republics of village panchayat and its higher territorial entitites.

New Delhi

D. Bandyopadhyay
Convenor.
Task Force on Panchayati Raj
Rajiv Gandhi Foundation
&
Dr. Amitava Mukherjee

Acknowledgments

The Rajiv Gandhi Foundation is thankful to the Ford Foundation for the financial support in bringing out this publication.

RGF is also thankful to the authors who contributed papers included in the publication viz., Shri Mani Shankar Aiyar, Prof. Y.K. Alagh, Shri D. Bandyopadhyay, Mrs. Nirmala Buch, Shri V. Ramachandran, Dr. Kumud Sharma and Shri B.N. Yugandhar.

RGF is also thankful to Dr. Amitava Mukherjee for undertaking the task of editing this publication as his labour of love. Foundation also thanks the editors of Economic and Political Weekly, Mumbai and Man & Development, Chandigarh for allowing two papers originally published in their journal, in this publication.

The editors are grateful to Shri Manmohan Malhoutra, Secretary-General, Shri O.P. Rehan and other members of the staff of the Rajiv Gandhi Foundation for the support they rendered to them in bringing out this publication.

New Delhi **D. Bandyopadhyay**

Contents

Introduction

D. Bandyopadhyay and *Dr. Amitava Mukherjee*

> *"The ultimate measure of a man is not where he stands in moments of comfort and conveniences but where he stands at times of challenge and controversy."*
>
> — Dr. Martin Luther King

The issue of good governance is, today, deemed central to development throughout the world. Not only is "good governance" a public good in itself to be guaranteed to people without exception, it is also accepted as a crucial variable for development to proceed along a sustainable path. Sustainability in this context is predicated upon equity and justice. Good governance has concurrently come to be seen at two planes. One, at the operational level, where good governance is described in terms of efficiency, absence of corruption in public life, accountability and transparency. Two, at the institutional plane, where good governance is perceived in the forms it takes: democratic, decentralised, participatory and operated by political incentives or its obverse, disincentives. Exercise of power by people's representatives in full view of the electors is a deterrance to gross abuse and misuse of authority.

Within the boundaries set by this paradigmatic shift and emergence of good governance as not only an imperative public good but a critical variable that drives the development process, panchayats occupy an unique position. At the institutional plane, they provide all the ingredients of good governance :

democratic, decentralised, participatory and clearly equilibrated by political incentives or disincentives. On the operational plane, it is less clear if panchayats have transparency, efficiency and absence of public thievery (not enumerated in any particular order) of the quality essential for good governance. Exactly a decade after the enactment of the 73rd and 74th Constitutional Amendment Acts, as one walks down the memory lane, probably one would find enough causes for cheers but the echo of those choruses would also be marred by numerous disappointments and frustrations.

Election in almost all the states to Panchayati Raj Institutions (PRIs), enactment of conformity Acts by all the states, extension of the institution of panchayats to Scheduled Areas, Constitution of State Finance Commissions, women taking an increasing role in panchayat governance (not withstanding at less than warranted levels) and implementation of some programmes of economic development financed by the Union Government do provide causes to celebrate. The first generation issues of panchayats not being held, Finance Commissions being given cold shoulders, women being only at the margin and the likes are no longer issues which agitate those who see panchayats as the instrumentality of good governance. Having surmounted these road blocks, focus of scrutiny has shifted to a host of new issues and new problems revolving around those issues.

The new issues have harassed the protagonists of panchayats and bolstered the skeptics. When the panchayats (in their new incarnation) were being formed, the celebration was that these were being elected, at all. Who ascended the power ladder was not much of a phenomenon to join issue with. After two rounds of elections it seems that intended benefits of PRIs have not flowed in to empower the truly disempowered : the poor, dalits, minorities, women, disabled, old-aged and socially marginalised groups in our societies. There is without doubt a continuum from Kerala and West Bengal forming the higher end of continuum and states like Bihar at the lowest end, nevertheless, the total picture is nothing to write home about. Capturing of PRIs by the elites has come about blatantly. Elites of every description have arrogated to themselves through money, muscle power, executive authority and bureaucratic clout (used either singly or jointly) powers that rightfully belong to the panchayats. Bandyopadhyay explores these issues which leave one wondering whether Ambedkar was prophetic when he positioned himself fully against the notion of village panchayats. He gives a succinct account of astonishing ways and means adopted by the legislators, bureaucracy and the rich to appropriate power to themselves sacrificing without demur or hesitation well down the road of decentralisation had provided for legislation that is germane to making serious inroads into the letter and spirit of the Constitution Amendment under reference.

The 73rd and 74th Constitutional Amendments were central Acts to establish the third tier of governments and the conformity Acts were state legislations. While the states legislated to create the PRIs, they were done under constitutional compulsion; the conformity Acts were not autonomous by the states to decentralise (noting, however, that some states like West Bengal and Kerala had a system of PRIs in place, irrespective of the Constitutional Amendments). While having conformity Acts in almost all the states was a big leap, the states had no compunction to encapsulate within the Acts expressed provisions which detracted away from the domain important chunks of authority and power. Buch in her paper has examined these legislative aberrations in different states. The intention of the state legislators and state governments have special provisions which were not consistent with the Constitutional Amendments under reference, may have been to provide for regional demands and create political spaces for entities within the states which were unique. However, in hindsight probably even they would not loath to accept that those legislative manouvering did not further the cause of PRIs. The legislative deviations pertain to organisation of representation and reservation in panchayats, devolution of powers and functions, establishment of District Planning Committees and trends in creation of alternative (read parallel) structures for developmental interventions by the state governments in areas covered by the Eleventh Schedule of the Constitution. For instance, Section 149 of Panchayati Raj Act of Andhra Pradesh enjoins for co-option of a person from the minority community in the Mandal Panchayat (Intermediary Panchayat) and Section 171 provides for co-option of two members of the minority community in the Zilla Parishad, both of which are in breach of Article 243 C (2) of the Constitution that all panchayat members will be directly elected from territorial constituencies. There are similar, though not identical, provisions in other State Panchayati Raj Acts such as in Punjab, West Bengal and Madhya Pradesh. Even in case of reservation for SCs/STs, there are significant variations from the constitutional mandate handed down to the states. In matters of finances, the route adopted by the states, apparently to delay devolution to the PRIs, was the executive route. For example, in Maharashtra while the State Finance Commission took 2 years and 9 months to file their report, the government took another 2 years and 2 months to table the report to the state legislature. Whatever the compulsions, these delays do not in any sense add to the credibility of the State Finance Commission and the good intentions of the state government. By not constituting the District Planning Committees (DPCs) for years and where constituted by changing the composition of the DPCs, the state governments have rendered Article 243 ZD infructuous or dysfunctional. In the process, the PRIs have been even more marginalised by robbing them of the opportunity of discharging their original functions of preparing plans for economic development and social justice under Article 243 G of the Constitution. When all these are added up, together with the creation of parallel structures (dealt with by Bandyopadhyay, Yugandhar and Mukherjee in this volume and hence not discussed here), the picture that comes to our mind in establishing the third tier of governance is an unhappy one. Though the motion of creating (or recreating) these institutions have all been gone through, the substance is missing. The "forms" are there, but not the content. Often the chaffs are without grain.

A unique feature of the new generation PRIs has been the

mandatory reservation of seats for women. The questions of social justice and gender justice were sought to be addressed in the Constitution through structural interventions: reservations and rotations. While the machinations by the governments in reservation for SCs/STs have been dealt with by Buch. Sharma has examined the issue from a purely women's perspective. Sharma notes how starting from adopting a minimalist approach the capacity building of women members of PRIs (as opposed to having an integrated approach); patriarchies of state, political parties and communities; misuse of legal provisions in abusing the provision for no-confidence motion; mandatory rotation of seats; issue of quorum in Gram Sabhas; disqualification of elected representatives on the basis of the number of children and lack of space to introduce new interests and concern, the women's issues have been marginalised. The presence of women elected representative is only symbolic, not substantive.

A reference is made in Buch's paper about parallel institutions being set up for the government-led development interventions to be administered and managed which lie within the purview of the PRIs. Bandyopadhyay, Yugandhar and Mukherjee argue that, given the progression of the self-help group (SHG), movement in different parts of the country, some sponsored by the state, some by cummunity-based organisations (CBOs) and NGOs, political and economic expediencies demand that their presence is recognised. Their continuance has to be preserved. SHGs are in fact a form of participatory democracy. For the greatest good of the communities involved, it is better to work out a synergy between the SHGs and the PRIs. To do so, representatives from the SHGs may be inducted into the Standing Committees (or analogous bodies) that the PRIs may have at different levels, so that various interest groups represented by the SHGs are represented within the panchayats. The SHGs can act as advocacy units, 'pressure points' or even implementing agencies for the PRIs. This scheme to work would need capacity building of the PRIs, of the SHG and convergence of development programmes. While convergence of programmes at the implementation plan can be achieved by working out a synergy between the PRIs and SHGs, convergence at the programming plane, can be achieved through re-establishing and/or revamping the decrepit planning at the district and sub-district levels, as the case may be. The issues are how to work out the synergy between the PRIs and SHGs on the one part, and of establishing an empowered planning system at the district and sub-district levels.

In a simple charter-like style, Ramachandran makes some significant points. He argues for power shedding not only by the states but also by the Centre in favour of panchayats. He suggests review of all Central and State laws which militate against genuine devolution of power and authority of PRIs. He objects to creation of parallel bodies/structures by the Centre and States which hinder proper functioning of panchayats. He recommends a greater role for the Comptroller & Auditor General for better financial management of panchayats. He suggests setting up of independent institutions to deal with finances of these bodies. He provides a mini-manual for good governance.

Alagh draws attention to a whole new set of institutions for rural development, with whom PRIs have to interface. He not only argues that community-based institutions with a sharp focus will have to be central to the next phase of rural development in India. Alagh positions the debate at the vertex of three issues : one, strategies for turning around of communities and individuals in fragile regions and at risk; two, policies for supporting these strategies; and three, nature of partnerships between different stakeholders when they do not understand each others' language. Socio-economic rules and incentives and disincentives have to be settled to guarantee that organisations and structures are in position to foster replicability of success stories.

With these new issues that confront the contemporary PRIs, there is need to re-examine what governments should do and cannot do. Aiyar has given a roadmap with milestones. He attempted at arguing for a set of measures that could mitigate some of the new issues discussed in this volume and others. Though these prescriptions have been suggested taking a broad view, they are robust. However, there may be a case for the states to modify these recommendations to meet state specific exigencies. That also explains why some of the recommendations of Aiyar's paper are at variance with the conclusions reached in the other papers. The attempt is to present a mosaic of views to stimulate debate and effective follow-up action to back up rhetoric.

The issues discussed in this volume are, by no means, exhaustive. There are other new issues as well which remain uncovered and must await another volume. For instance, all the issues revolving around social restructuring in order to facilitate the entry and acceptance of women, the scheduled castes and scheduled tribes in PRIs have to be carefully scrutinized afresh. Participative democracy cannot be legislated. Social mores and structures must be remodelled to allow free and full participation by those who eke out a life at the margins of society. Then again, the entire issue of right to information at and from the Gram Panchayat level needs to be given a serious consideration, not merely as a weapon to eradicate corruption at the village level, but as a creative exercise in government for the people, by the people. Means to secure informations, such as public hearing, is a small but significant step towards the transition from representative democracy to participative democracy. It is hoped that newer issues will be addressed sooner than later, though many of them may be controversial. But controversy ought not to deter the powers that be to put the panchayats on the fast track.

1

Towards Time-bound Panchayati Raj

Tenth Anniversary Plan of Action

Mani Shankar Aiyar

INTRODUCTION

It is ten years since Parliament incorporated Part IX ("The Panchayats") and Part IXA ("The Municipalities") into the Constitution.

A measure of success has been achieved in bringing state legislation everywhere in conformity with the mandatory provisions of Parts IX and IXA.

Once elections are held in Arunachal Pradesh, Jharkhand and Pondicherry, the process of establishing elected local bodies in all areas of the country – rural and urban – would have been accomplished. Indeed, many states have had a second round of Panchayat/municipal elections since the Constitution was amended.

Moreover, the system of reservations has been implemented everywhere. Of around 30 lakh elected local bodies' representatives, around ten lakh are women. They also occupy a third of all chairpersonships at all three tiers of the Panchayat system and the municipalities. Schduled castes/Scheduled tribes representation in the local bodies, at both membership and chairmanship levels, is in proportion to their population. Most state legislatures have made provision for reservations for the other backward classes. With Panchayati Raj having been made irreversible, we have moved some way institutionally towards making India not only the world's largest democracy but also the world's most representative democracy. This is an achievement of far-reaching significance.

However, much remains to be accomplished about actually empowering the elected local bodies to function as "institutions of local self-government" – the key provision of Article 243G of Part IX and of Article 243W of Part IXA which define the over-arching goal of effective Panchayati Raj. The record here is very mixed, and largely disappointing. A few states have made notable progress towards Panchayati Raj in substance. Most have not. What is now needed, in this tenth anniversary year of constitutionally obligated Panchayati Raj, is a stock-taking of the experience of all states which will enable us to chart a road-map for the time-bound implementation of the vision of the Constitution. It is suggested that such time-bound implementation be secured within a period of the next five years (2003-08).

DRAFT ROAD-MAP (2003-2008)

1. Effective Devolution

(i) The Eleventh and Twelfth Schedules to the Constitution indicate, respectively, the 29 and 18 subjects in respect of which functions might be devolved to the Panchayati Raj Institutions (PRIs) and the municipalities. Most state legislations provide for all the subjects listed in the two Schedules to be devolved to the elected local bodies. Some states have added other subjects to the list. It is to be emphasized that the two Schedules are illustrative in nature; states are free to expand the list to include other subjects.

(ii) Effective devolution requires not only the devolution of functions but also the devolution of functionaries and finances. Not until functions, functionaries and finances are all devolved can there be effective devolution. The number of subjects listed for devolution is less important than securing effective devolution of functions related to these subjects. States may, therefore, prepare a five-year plan for effective devolution, aimed at accomplishing full devolution of functions, functionaries and finances for all devolved subjects in pre-determined annual stages over the next five years.

(iii) Devolution should be based on the principle of "subsidiarity", that is, whatever can be accomplished at a lower level should be entrusted to that level. Only that which cannot be effectively implemented at a lower tier might be taken to a higher tier.

(iv) Devolution may also be made irreversible: a function once devolved should not be arbitrarily taken back. Therefore, it would be preferable to make provision for devolution through legislation rather than administrative orders.

(v) For devolution to the PRIs, there should be a clear demarcation subject-wise of functions devolved to each of the three tiers of the PRIs. Such demarcation would be essential in determining the contingent devolution of functionaries and finances to each of the three tiers of the system. Technically, this is called 'activity mapping'. A working group of the Union Ministry of Rural Development has undertaken a detailed illustrative exercise in activity mapping. Based on that model, states should initiate activity mapping within calendar year 2003 with the aim of completing the exercise as soon as possible and in any case by the end of 2004 at the latest.

(vi) Effective devolution is not a one-way street where states at their discretion determine the degree and nature of devolution. It should be a symbiotic process involving dialogue with the elected local bodies. To this end, empowered Panchayats/Municipal Councils may be established by 2004 at the latest in all states/UTs to provide an institutional framework for joint consideration by elected local bodies' representatives and state governments of all issues relating to the legitimate entitlements of the Panchayati Raj

Institutions and Municipalities as set out in the Constitution and state legislation.

2. Finances

(i) A decade after the passage of the Constitution amendments, Panchayats/municipalities at all levels are starved of finances in almost all states. Responsibility without powers or means is discrediting Panchayati Raj almost everywhere, leaving many elected members of the local bodies frustrated with little or nothing to do. The "sound finances" of the Panchayats/municipalities is a constitutional obligation enjoined by Article 243I and 243Y, respectively.

(ii) Therefore, as an integral part of activity mapping, the quantum of finances that will be made available on a five-year and annual basis to the Panchayats/ municipalities at each level must be indicated as unambiguously as possible. On the basis of the experience gathered hitherto, and their respective road maps for effective devolution, states must give urgent attention to letting the elected local bodies know what they might expect by way of tied and untied grants, as well as what resources they are expected to raise on their own. This exercise must be initiated immediately and completed as early as possible. With effect from fiscal year 2004-2005, state budgets must clearly indicate what sums of money under what heads, tied and untied, are being made available to which elected local bodies. This is already being done in some states.

(iii) Simultaneously, the central government may be urged to ensure that all moneys for programmes related to functions devolved in terms of the Eleventh and Twelfth Schedules – estimated at Rs. 31,000 crore per annum, is channlled direct to the Panchayats/ municipalities at the appropriate level. This will preclude diversion, temporary or permanent, to ways and means expenditure or other uses of the financial entitlements of the elected local bodies. The central government, for its part, will have to consider restructuring its own planning and implementation mechanisms and monitoring agencies to ensure there is no centralization in the name of decentralization. Central and centrally-sponsored schemes should be so conceived and executed as to promote and not impede effective devolution and the larger constitutional purposes of elected local bodies functioning as institutions of local self-government.

(iv) Moreover, finances devolved to the Panchayats/ municipalities by the state or central governments must be managed and administered by the elected bodies themselves and not resumed for planning, implementation or expenditure by para-statal bodies or parallel structures.

(v) The Centre must ensure the strict monitoring of Finance Commission grants to the elected local bodies as this is a constitutionally mandatory requirement.

(vi) State Finance Commission's, recommendations are recommendatory not mandatory in nature, but once they are accepted by the state legislature, implementation must follow. Unfortunately, there are many states where the pace of implementation of State Finance Commission's recommendations has lagged far behind their acceptance by the state legislature. State governments may be urged to undertake a review of the state of implementation of all accepted recommendations. Consideration may also be given in establishing a standing committee of the state legislature to keep a watch on the "sound finances" of the elected local bodies, particularly with a view to supervising and monitoring the progress in implementing Central and State Finance Commission's recommendations.

(vii) Elected local bodies cannot function as "institutions

of local self-government" until they are endowed with substantial untied funds which they can spend not as directed by the central/state government but as determined by the Panchayats/municipalities in consultation with Gram/Ward Sabhas.

(viii) Moreover, fiscal responsibility will evolve only when local bodies are empowered and obliged to complement grants received by raising their own finances through taxation, particularly forms of taxation which enable the local bodies, in accordance with the provisions of Articles 243H and 243X, to "appropriate" the revenues so raised for their own purposes instead of being obliged to credit them to the consolidated fund. District Panchayats and municipalities may also be encouraged and assisted in raising funds through bond issues.

(ix) States may, therefore, prepare a road-map by the end of the fiscal year 2003-04 for untying as large a proportion of grants to the Panchayats/municipalities as possible, and the Centre may be urged to follow the suit. State Finance Commissions may be requested to pay particular attention to augmenting the fiscal self-reliance of the elected local bodies.

3. Functionaries

(i) Democracy requires the subordination of the bureaucracy to the elected representatives. This applies as much to the third level of governance through the elected local bodies as it does to governance at the level of the state or Union government.

(ii) It is, therefore, essential that District Rural Development Authorities (DRDAs) be abolished and merged with the district Panchayat (Zila Parishad) under the chairpersonship of the district Panchayat chairperson.

(iii) Functionaries posted to the PRIs/municipalities must

be brought under the authority and discipline of the elected bodies. Progressively, states should build a cadre of bureaucrats and technocrats who would be constituted into Panchayats/Municipalities Service.

(iv) PRIs/municipalities must be left free to determine the number of bureaucrats/technocrats on their rolls so as to free them of the financial overburden of excess staff which plagues state governments

(v) At present, the decisions and functioning of PRIs/municipalities are subject to review by bureaucratic authorities who are often empowered to over-rule the elected authority. States may move towards a system of peer review, where it is the Panchayat at the higher level, rather than the bureaucracy, which reviews and rectifies errors at the lower level. Where decisions of the district Panchayat require review, a standing committee of the legislature may be constituted to undertake this task. For the municipalities, a parallel system of peer review may be put in place. Of course, since the minister is ultimately responsible to the legislature for the elected local bodies, he must remain the authority of last resort on matters that are not resolved at lower levels.

4. Planning

(i) Many states are still to fulfil their mandatory constitutional obligation to constitute District Planning Committees (DPCs) in accordance with the procedure set out in Article 243 ZD of Part IXA of the Constitution. As this amounts to a serious violation of constitutional provisions, it is essential that DPCs be duly constituted in every district. Calendar year 2003 may be set as the last and final year for the accomplishment of this constitutional obligation.

(ii) Few states have demonstrated adequate awareness of the centrality accorded by the Constitution to planning at the grassroots level. "The preparation of plans for economic development and social justice" is the key functional obligation devolved on the Panchayats/ municipalities as "institutions of self-government" by Articles 243G and 243W, respectively.

(iii) Such planning is required constitutionally to be undertaken at each level of the PRIs, including separately the village Panchayat, the intermediate panchayat and the district Panchayat. Similarly, Nagar Panchayats and municipalities are required to prepare their own plans. The "consolidation" of all these separate plans — of the Panchayats and the municipalities — is required to be undertaken by the DPC, as set out in Article 243ZD. The consolidated district plan is then to be forwarded to the state authority. Consideration may be given to the convening of a general assembly of all Panchayat/ municipality representatives to endorse the plan consolidated by the DPC so as to strengthen the democratic credentials of the DPC plan for integration into the state plan. Such detailed district planning according to the constitutional schema is being undertaken virtually nowhere. A five-year road-map, with annual milestones, for effective participatory district planning in each state is thus an imperative need.

(iv) District plans are a vital input for effective state planning, even as state plans are a crucial input for national-level planning. Therefore, the national goal should be to ensure that the Eleventh Plan commencing in 2007 is firmly anchored in district plans prepared by the DPCs according to the constitutional mandate.

(v) The constitutional mandate stipulates that planning by the elected local bodies shall be subject to such conditions as may be laid down by the state legislatures. Before the commencement of fiscal year 2003-04, states may please ensure that adequate legislative provision is made for effective district planning. Such legislative provision may pay particular attention to the requirements of "social justice" stipulated in the Constitution. This is essential to ensure that the weaker sections, including women, are fully benefited by and not discriminated against in the process of grassroots planning.

(vi) Effective planning also requires that elected local bodies at every level have a fair idea of the resources that will be available to them on an annual and five-year basis, as also a clear idea of the resources they can raise and retain on their own. State governments need to ensure that this information is made available to each elected local body. The resources availability should also be clearly and categorically provided for in state budgets.

(vii) The key to participatory planning lies in mobilizing the local community to articulate their priorities in an informed and intelligent manner so that grassroots planning moves from being the preparation of a wish-list into a feasible, responsible plan. To this end, the Gram Sabha, or better still, the ward/neighbourhood Sabha is where the process must begin.

(viii) Planning at the Gram Sabha/Ward Sabha level should be preceded and accompanied by an awareness campaign mounted by activists drawn from the local community and civil society generally so that the community is conscientized about the significance of grassroots planning for their own welfare and development.

(ix) Moreover, professionally qualified and experienced elements of the local community (serving and retired) should be mobilized and co-opted into rationally assessing and explaining the alternatives to the people to facilitate informed choice by the local community.

(x) Each state may, in association with civil society representatives, make arrangements within calendar year 2003 for launching such a people's movement.

(xi) The Planning Commission, for its part, must recognize

that it can and must play a crucial role in encouraging grassroots planning by insisting on the district plan components before sanctioning the annual state plans.

5. Implementation of Programmes

(i) As "institutions of local self-government", PRIs at all three levels and the municipalities are required, under Article 243G and Article 243W respectively, to undertake the "implementation of programmes of economic development and social justice." Progress in this regard has been most inadequate in most states. This is partly because paper devolution has not been accompanied by effective devolution, but largely because even where PRIs/municipalities are involved in implementation, they function more as implementation agencies of government programmes than as "institutions of local self-government".

(ii) A key element of effective implementation must be the restructuring of line departments into no more than secretariat offices as part and parcel of the effective devolution of functions, and related functionaries and finances, to the Panchayats/municipalities.

(iii) Retaining line departments, while apparently devolving planning and implementation to the elected local bodies, has forestalled Panchayats/municipalities from evolving into "institutions of local self-government". Worse, the nexus established between the bureaucracy and the chairpersons of the PRIs/municipalities has fostered widespread corruption, leading to the defaming and discrediting of the Panchayati Raj system as a whole. It is essential that the nexus between the chairpersons of the PRIs/municipalities and the local bureaucracy, arising out of elected local bodies being converted into implementation agencies of the state government, be broken. The restructuring of line departments for devolved subjects will not only subordinate the bureaucracy to the elected authority, it will forestall implementation being perverted into the chairperson and the bureaucracy sharing the spoils.

(iv) Chairpersons of local bodies must function as chairpersons-in-council, taking the consent of the general body of the Panchayat/municipality for all decisions. To this end, not only must the elected local body as a whole, and not just the chairperson, is the implementing authority, the Gram/Ward/neighbourhood Sabha must be deeply and continuously involved in the process. Concurrent social audit is the most effective check on corruption.

(v) Effective implementation requires the participation of all members of the Panchayat/municipality at each level through subjects committees that will manage the implementation; jointly call for tenders, examine bids and, with the consent of all concerned, award contracts; and undertake collegiate supervision by the concerned subject committee as a whole of the implementation of works so that there is complete satisfaction before payments are made.

(vi) The role of the Gram/Ward Sabhas in this regard is crucial. Programmes undertaken by Panchayats should initially be approved by Gram/Ward Sabhas; utilisation certificates must statutorily require prior Gram Sabha approval; and beneficiary identification must be done transparently in the presence of all members of the Gram/Ward Sabha.

(vii) States may prepare road-maps for effective time-bound implementation arrangements along these lines by the end of calendar year 2003. Sanctions against wrongdoings, through a carrot-and-stick system of checks and balances to curb corrupt practices should be built into such road maps.

6. Gram Sabhas

(i) Unlike the first two tiers of governance – the state and the centre – PRIs/municipalities do not have legislatures to act as a check and a break on the executive authority. In the Panchayati Raj system, that role of advice and consent has to be performed by the Gram Sabhas functioning effectively as people's parliaments. Weak or ineffective Gram Sabhas fuel corruption and social discrimination. A strong system of Gram Sabhas is thus the foundation of good governance through Panchayati Raj.

(ii) The size of the Gram Sabha varies from state to state and even within states. Experience has shown that the larger the Gram Sabha the less effective it is and the more liable to capture by the dominant elements in the Panchayat area. The answer to this lies in ward/neighbourhood Sabhas for populations of around 200-300 so that all elements of the local community are able to articulate their concerns. Some states have already made such arrangements. Others may reinforce their Gram Sabhas by establishing ward/neighbourhood sabhas, as appropriate, by the end of calendar year 2004 but preferably during 2003 itself.

(iii) Attendance at Gram Sabha meetings has been thin and declining virtually everywhere. Villagers do not feel they are stakeholders in the Gram Sabha because the role and functions of the Gram Sabha are inadequate, even non-existent. Gram sabha meetings have thus been reduced to a meaningless ritual, primarily aimed at rubber-stamping decisions and work undertaken without full consultations with the Gram Sabha. For the meaningful empowerment of the Gram/Ward Sabhas, they must be entitled to all the informations required for transparent and good governance, as well as given duties which would make the elected Panchayat answerable to the gram/ward sabha. At a minimum, Gram/Ward Sabhas should be empowered to approve all plans and programmes for economic development and social justice before implementation begins; be entitled to authorize the issue or withholding of utilization certificates for funds allocated to different projects/programmes of the Panchayat; and given full powers for the identification of beneficiaries for beneficiary-oriented poverty alleviation programmes.

(iv) The participation of women in Gram/Ward Sabha meetings has been woeful. To rectify this, Mahila Sabhas, comprising all adult women voters, should be organized at Gram/Ward level so that they can discuss among themselves issues coming before the larger meeting and authorize from among themselves spokespersons (or *saathins*) who will speak for the Mahila Sabha at the Panchayat and Gram Sabha levels.

(v) Within the calendar year 2003, legislative and other steps may be taken to ensure that the powers and responsibilities of the Gram/Ward Sabhas are spelt out and Mahila Sabhas begin functioning.

(vi) Parallel arrangements for the municipalities may also be made within the prescribed time-frame.

7. Women

(i) In many states, a disproportionate number of no-confidence motions are being moved against women chairpersons with the ulterior objective of replacing them with men. To forestall such malpractice, states may make immediate provision in their laws to ensure that if a woman chairperson is removed for want of confidence, her place can be taken only by another woman.

(ii) Although in an increasing number of states, women are showing themselves capable of standing and winning from general seats, by and large, it is reservations that are responsible for nearly one lakh women holding elective position in the Panchayats/

municipalities. The Constitution has left it to the states to decide the frequency of rotation of seats reserved for women. On the basis of their own experience and of others, states are requested to undertake a thorough review of the functioning of rotations and introduce appropriate reforms before the next round of Panchayat/municipal elections.

8. Reservations for Scheduled Castes/Tribes

The system of reservations, as it is being implemented, needs serious review and revamping to bring it in line with the constitutional provisions. Articles 243D and 243T, relating respectively to the Panchayats and municipalities, clearly state that the number of seats to be reserved in any Panchayat/municipal area should be related to the proportion of SC/ST population "in that Panchayat/municipal area." However, almost all states have instead taken the state average for SC/ST and reserved that proportion of seats/posts on a rough-and-ready basis, leading to anomalies like SC/ST chairpersons in Panchayats/municipalities where SC/ST representation is small and general category chairpersons in Panchayats/municipalities where the SC/ST presence is strong. This also leads to demands for rotation. Rotation of SC/ST seats is not provided for in the Constitution because the constitutional scheme envisaged reservations not on the basis of the ratio of population in the state but the ratio in each Panchayat at that level, as well as in the municipal areas on that same basis. States may, therefore, take a fresh look at the system of reservations to bring their respective systems in consonance with the constitutional schema.

9. Special Problems of SC/ST

(i) It was the apprehension of villages being "cesspools" of social discrimination and prejudice that most inhibited Babasaheb Dr. B.R. Ambedkar from according a high place in the Constitution to Panchayati Raj as the foundation of our democracy.

(ii) It was to take into account the very real danger of PRIs and even municipalities being misused to institutionalize discrimination and empower the elite at the expense of the ordinary citizen that, when the Constitution was amended to incorporate Parts IX and IXA on the Panchayats and the Municipalities, apart from reservations for the weaker sections, "social justice" was explicitly integrated with economic development as integral to the planning and implementation functions of elected local bodies as "institutions of local self-government."

(iii) State governments need to recognize, as most in any case do, that constitutional and legal measures for social justice might set the stage but it is at the grassroots level that the closest vigilance has to be maintained. Therefore, in addition to concurrent social audit by Gram/Ward Sabhas, which is the most effective way of checking prejudice and discrimination, DPCs may exercise due diligence to ensure that the social justice component is integrated into all development plans and social welfare schemes; that social justice committees are established at all three levels in the PRIs as well as in the municipalities; that a grievance redressal machinery is built into the framework of the Panchayati Raj system; and that encouragement is given to the weaker sections to articulate their grievances in Gram/Ward Sabha meetings.

(iv) With regard to ST communities, the single biggest problem they are facing is the non-sensitive, non-humanitarian way in which central and state forest conservation Acts are being used to oust and displace tribal communities without adequate regard for the integral relationship between the *vanvasis* and the forests in which, or on the edge of which, they live. This calls for a thorough time-bound review by all states of the adverse, if unintended, consequences of the way in which forest conservation – in itself an important goal – is being implemented on the ground. It is equally necessary that forest development agencies function under the aegis of the Panchayats in tribal areas in strict accord with the provisions of PESA – The Provisions of Panchayats (Extension to Scheduled Areas) Act, 1996 (see the next point below).

(v) For Fifth Schedule areas, Article 243M (3) (b) provides that it is not state legislatures but Parliament which will enact the Panchayati Raj legislation. To this end, Parliament has passed the Provisions of Panchayats (Extension to Scheduled Areas) Act, 1996 [PESA], based on the Bhuria Committee recommendations. (A draft Bill, under Article 243ZC (3) (b) for Municipal areas in Fifth Schedule areas has been introduced in Parliament and referred to the Standing Committee on Urban and Rural Development.) PESA is an excellent Act, but is hardly being implemented, uniformly or strictly, in any Fifth Schedule area. A road-map for the time-bound implementation of the Act is essential on the part of all states incorporating Fifth Schedule areas. Such a road-map may be prepared as early as possible and in any case not later than the end of 2004.

(vi) The juridical position in regard to states incorporating only Fifth Schedule areas (e.g. Chhattisgarh and Jharkhand) needs clarification. In such states, does the Act of Parliament prevail over state legislation or is there scope for state legislation to substitute an Act of Parliament passed as per the mandate of the Constitution?

(vii) Even if it is in accordance with the law and Constitution for Fifth Schedule states to enact their own legislation, such states are urged to incorporate in their legislation the PESA provisions in respect of the empowerment and functions of the Gram Sabhas, as also tribal community rights over natural, mineral and forest resources specified in the central Act. With this in mind, states concerned may undertake a time-bound review of their extant legislation.

10. Elections

(i) Although the Constitution provides for elections before the expiry of five years of the first meeting of the elected local bodies, there have been serious delays in many states in the conduct of timely elections. The Supreme Court has laid down the exceptional circumstances in which a slight delay may be condoned as unavoidable, but the practice of delaying elections on other grounds has become regrettably widespread. This is as true of elections as of bye-elections.

(ii) The Constitution stipulates in Articles 243E (4) and 243U (4), respectively, that if a Panchayat/municipality is dissolved for any reason, elections must be held within six months to reconstitute that particular Panchayat/municipality. This provision is being widely misused to dissolve all Panchayats/municipalities and then avail of the six-months provision to not hold elections at all.

(iii) States must commit themselves to holding elections within the stipulated time-period subject only to the exceptional conditions set out in the Supreme Court order.

(iv) Complaints of electoral malpractice are widespread. State Election Commissions, in consultation with the central Election Commission, may consider ways and means of ridding local bodies' elections of electoral malpractice.

11. Audit

(i) The audit of the accounts of elected local bodies has generally been so tardy and haphazard as to have virtually ceased to have practical effect in ensuring the integrity of PRIs/municipalities.

(ii) State Auditors-General, in consultation with the Auditor & Comptroller General of India, may be advised to urgently identify and correct deficiencies in this regard.

12. Parallel Bodies

(i) Once devolution of any subject or range of subjects receives the approval of the legislature by the passage of the required state legislation, setting up parallel programmes, like Janmabhoomi in Andhra Pradesh, to run through "nodal officers" programmes which stand constitutionally and legally devolved to the PRIs/municipalities, or parastatal bodies to administer functions and finances devolved to the local bodies, constitutes a travesty of the Constitution and the law, and undermines the purposes for which the Constitution was amended by the 73rd and 74th amendments. As such, all parallel programmes and parallel parastatal bodies should be wound up and no fresh ones started. Functions (and related finances) devolved to the PRIs/municipalities must be exercised solely through the elected local bodies.

(ii) As regards bodies like Parents-Teachers Associations and Water Users Association, their legitimacy may be recognized but they must be brought under the overall aegis of the PRIs/municipalities and not left to function as parallel bodies outside the Panchayati Raj system. In particular, forest development agencies must function under the overall aegis of the panchayats in accordance with the provisions of PESA.

(iii) The practice of appointing bureaucrats or ministers as chairpersons of the DPCs needs to be discouraged as this tends to convert DPCs into parallel bodies. Moreover, as district plans, according to the Constitution (Articles 243G and W respectively), have to conform to the "conditions" stipulated by the state legislature and have, in any case, to be submitted to the state authority, it is in the state capital and not at the district level that ministers and state governments should have their say. Therefore, to ensure that DPCs reflect the consensus of the elected local bodies rather than perspectives imposed from outside, the chairpersonship of the DPC should invariably vest in the chairperson of the district Panchayat chairperson.

(iv) Equally, planning mechanisms which second-guess or substitute the functions of the DPCs at the district level must be wound up forthwith as they are subversive of elected local bodies fulfilling their constitutional role as institutions of local self-government.

13. Capacity-Building and Training

(a) In association with specialist academic institutions and experts, NGOs, and civil society in general, state governments need to embark on a sustained programme of capacity-building and training at all levels from the Gram/Mahila Sabha and the elected local bodies (especially women and the weaker sections of society) to the DPCs and the bureaucracy at all levels, extending to MPs and MLAs, to optimize the working of Panchayati Raj to the benefit of all.

(b) Distance education, which has a particularly important role to play in training and the multimedia programmes devised by the Indira Gandhi National Open University, deserves particular attention. Indeed, the electronic media constitutes the single most cost-effective method of reaching large numbers of those concerned with the best available training talent in the state and country.

14. MPs/MLAs

(i) Panchayati Raj purists argue that just as members of the elected bodies are not involved in the work of the Assemblies/Parliament, so also it is illegitimate to involve MLAs/MPs in the work of the elected local bodies.

(ii) While there is merit to this point in terms of the separation of jurisdictions, the ground reality is that even as MPs and MLAs occupy the same geographical and electoral space and, therefore, cannot be excluded from each other's domains, so also MPs and MLAs have of necessity to share the same constituency space and constituents' concerns as members of the elected local bodies. It may also be noted that although PRIs/ municipalities are envisaged as "institutions of local self-government", they are executive bodies and not legislative authorities of the kind that MPs/MLAs are elected to.

(iii) Therefore, instead of undermining Panchayati Raj itself by promoting a conflict of interests between MPs/MLAs, on the one hand, and PRI/municipality members/chairpersons, on the other, it might be best to facilitate arrangements, as provided for in the Constitution, whereby MPs/MLAs are associated with the work of the PRIs/municipalities without, however, becoming part of the decision-making process or transgressing the executive functions of the elected local bodies.

15. Jurisprudence

(i) Numerous cases relating to the interpretation of the constitutional and legal provisions of Panchayati Raj have been referred to the High Courts and the Supreme Court. The Supreme Court is already engaged in harmonizing the jurisprudence in this regard as there appears to be variations in judicial pronouncements on aspects of Panchayati Raj. A clear and consistent body of jurisprudence is essential for the full and proper implementation of the constitutional provisions in accordance with the letter and spirit of the 73rd and 74th amendments.

(ii) It was the legislative practice in British India to attach a Local Government Memorandum to draft legislation (as is the practice now with the Financial Memorandum) to ensure that legislation was in conformity with the devolved powers of local bodies. It would be appropriate to revive this practice.

(iii) The Constitution requires that extant legislation be reviewed to ensure that nothing in that legislation contravenes the provisions of Parts IX and IXA of the Constitution. However, virtually no state government has undertaken this exercise. It is recommended that the Law Commissions of the centre and the states be requested to study the matter and action be taken thereafter expeditiously.

16. State of the Panchayats/Municipalities Report

(i) To facilitate informed review and appraisal by the state legislature, Parliament and civil society/public opinion in general, the presentation of an annual status of Panchayats/Municipalities Report, perhaps in conjunction with the annual budget, should become standard practice by the commencement of fiscal year 2004-05.

(ii) As in the case of the Human Development Index, pioneered by the United Nations Development Programme but adopted by many state governments since, the core of the annual State of the Panchayats/Municipalities Report might be a Devolution Index which would enable a ready measure to be made of the progress in promoting development through empowerment.

(iii) The Planning Commission in New Delhi might consider preparing a nation-wide Devolution Index, which would enable states to consider further progress based on the best practice obtaining in the nation.

2

Panchayati Raj

Do's and Don'ts

V. Ramachandran

GOVERNMENT OF INDIA

Do's

- Decentralisation should be seen as a basic constitutionally-mandated governance reform and be given as much, if not more, importance than now being given to public sector reforms, fiscal reforms, power reforms, etc.,
- There should be a single ministry for local governments at the national level with a clear mandate for strengthening local governments. This ministry could deal with centrally sponsored anti-poverty and social infrastructure schemes.
- All ministries dealing with subjects in the domain of PRIs should have a PRI Cell, which interacts with the nodal ministry dealing with local governments.
- Avoid centrally sponsored schemes (CSS) in areas which are the legitimate domain of PRIs. Wherever CSS are inevitable due to priority or pilot nature, the guidelines issued by the ministries should give predominant specific roles to PRIs.
- Issue instructions to disband parallel bodies like DRDAs, FFDAs, BFDAs, various Health Societies, etc.

and give up the plans to set up new agencies like Forest Development Agency outside the PRI system. If for functional reasons an institutional set-up is needed, it should be under the PRI system with proper linkages.

- The guidelines for preparation of the Eleventh Five Year Plan should include clear roles for PRIs and the DPC. Since bottom up planning would take some time, the process could be started from the 3rd year of the Tenth Five Year Plan.
- Incentives should be given to states which strengthen PRIs. For this a Decentralisation Index could be constructed using experts and the states ranked by an independent agency.
- Funds flow under centrally sponsored schemes should be linked to the degree of empowerment of PRIs.
- It should be recognised that it is incumbent on the Central Government to devolve resources to local governments from the Central kitty through the Finance Commission Awards. The present arrangements are of a token nature. Devolution should be based on the division of responsibilities as per the Constitution between the state and local governments. The Twelfth Finance Commission should be specifically asked to look into this.
- The state should be encouraged to sponsor externally assisted projects to strengthen and institutionalise PRIs and such projects should be given preference while recommending for external assistance.
- Set apart at least 2 per cent of CSS funds for capacity building of local governments, including accounting and audit (see below).
- Restructure all statistics systems including census to bring them in harmony with PRI boundaries.
- Present an annual Status Report on PRIs in the country in the Parliament along with the budget.
- Institute national awards for three best performing panchayats at each level to be selected by an

independent jury from among the applicants.

- Set up a training network for PRIs by linking the best institutions in the country and assigning specific roles and responsibilities to each institution.
- Planning Commission and the ministry concerned should document best practices and disseminate them on a regular basis. Journals like *Yojana* and *Kurukshetra* should devote atleast one-third of their space for matters related to Panchayati Raj.
- Based on the experience of 10 years after obtaining feedback from the well-performing states, a consensus decision may be taken for making certain key amendments which, among other things, could provide for :
  - Elected District Government (instead of District Panchayat);
  - Taxes in the local government domain;
  - Audit control by C&AG; and
  - Setting up of independent systems for dealing with malfeasance of PRIs, hearing of appeals against decisions of PRIs, conduct of audit at the state level, etc.
- Merge and reduce the size of ministries/departments dealing with subjects listed in the 11th and 12th Schedules of the Constitution.
- Amend all Central Acts related to subjects in the 11th and 12th Schedules of the Constitution.
- Introduce a system for studying the local government implications of every government policy or legislation in future and publish the findings for general debate or for discussion in the Parliament as the case may be.

Don'ts

- Don't confine local government matters to just one ministry. Just as every ministry, dealing with subjects in the concurrent or State list, looks after States, it should also look after local governments in respect of its subject areas.

- Don't allow externally supported projects to spawn user groups and other community based organisations delinked from the PRI system.
- Do not give discretionary development powers to MPs. Abolish MPLADs.

STATE GOVERNMENTS

Do's

- Develop a vision of setting up institutions of local self government as envisaged in the Constitution and come out with a phased programme, not exceeding 10 years, to actualise it.
- Use decentralisation to bring in fundamental governance reforms like enhanced people's participation, citizen orientation, responsiveness, service delivery, improved financial management, accountability, and so on.
- Play an active role in handholding the process of decentralisation without directing or controlling it and also work out the withdrawal steps.
- Bring out a legislation which clearly defines functions of PRIs at each level and not just lists out subjects.
- Amend all legislations dealing with subject areas in terms of Article 253N of the Constitution *i.e.* any provision of pre-existing legislation (or post-73rd/74th Amendment) which do not conform to or are repugnants to the letter and spirit of Chapters IX and IX A should be modified/deleted as appropriate.
- Amend the business rules of the State legislature to make it mandatory for each Bill presented before the legislature to be accompanied by a memorandum on implications for local governments.
- Acts should be followed up with the software required

for operationalising them like Rules, Government Orders, Manuals, Circulars, and so on.

- The role range in respect of each subject for each PRI should be clearly spelt out and this role itself could be envisaged to change over a period of time; for example, in education it could start with managing of schools and later move on to recruiting of teachers, laying down their terms and conditions, subject to an overall framework and even preparing local variants to a core syllabus.
- Transfer works to PRIs along with workers. To start with, existing functionaries may be transferred. The question of performing the functions in future also needs to be addressed—the personnel, mode of recruitment, terms and conditions, etc.
- PRIs should control the staff working under them.
- There should be a clear policy on placement of staff transferred to PRIs.
- Funds required to perform the roles assigned to PRIs may be determined and transferred in an untied form to them.
- Funds to be transferred to PRIs should be budgeted separately and devolved based on transparent formula.
- The availability of funds over a period of five years should be made clear so as to ensure predictability.
- PRIs should be given resource raising powers both tax and non-tax. Only the lower limit needs be set by the Government.
- There should be legal provision on fiscal responsibility of PRIs dealing with assessment and collection of revenue, borrowing mode of incurring expenditure, transparency, accountability, etc.
- Allow local governments to prepare schemes and plans locally.
- Control of local governments should only be through independent audit system.
- Provide for an auxiliary audit system which focuses

on concurrent help and correction to PRIs rather than post facto fault finding.

- Evolve a code of conduct governing the relationship between elected functionaries and officials.
- Redefine the role of the District Collector bringing it in line with the PRI system – for example, as Member Secretary of the DPC.
- As part of capacity building, help successful PRIs to share their experience with others.
- Select "beacon" panchayats through a transparent and independent process and give larger freedom to them to develop replicable models of development and / or governance.
- To prevent re-centralisation, introduce a legislative provision which makes it mandatory for every power being withdrawn from PRIs to get the approval of the proposed State Development Council and then the legislature.
- Provide special mechanisms for socially backward people to participate in the PRI system like special Gram Sabhas, reservation of funds, social audit etc.
- Set up an empowered committee to sort out operational problems during the process of decentralisation.
- Set up independent institutions to deal with malfeasance by PRIs to hear appeals against decision of PRIs etc.
- Launch a mobilisation campaign to give a push to decentralisation and set the agenda for the future.
- Create space for NGOs, CBOs and other civil society organisations to work in harmony with PRIs without affecting their legitimate position.
- Provide for participatory structures at all levels to bring in maximum people's participation in local governance.
- Give full freedom to local governments, but insist on following norms and due processes while taking decisions.

- Redefine the role of parastatals dealing with functions transferred to PRIs and bring in arrangements for them to work with PRIs as technical support agencies. Also, downsize them in a phased manner.
- Introduce provisions for right to information, social audit etc. in laws relating to PRIs.
- Announce a clear capacity building policy for local governments with definite operational strategy and resource commitments.
- Facilitate PRIs to outsource professional and technical support.
- Set up a State Development Council to discuss policy issues relating to decentralisation.

Don'ts

- Don't take away powers given to PRIs under one law through another law by introducing a "notwith-standing" clause.
- Avoid dual control of staff transferred to PRIs.
- Don't make PRIs miniature state governments by downloading the same procedures and systems to them.
- Withdraw from areas where powers have been given to PRIs.
- Totally give up discretionary grants for "need based" or "demand based" development programmes which are not transparent.
- Don't allow parallel schemes and parallel set-ups.
- Don't control PRIs through officials, especially the District Collector.
- Don't pit community-based organisations, NGOs against PRIs.
- Don't provide discretionary fund to MLAs.
- Don't make MPs and MLAs members of PRIs. Give up the system of Minister in charge of any district or DPC.
- Don't retain powers with state government to interface with decisions of PRIs to taxation and other matters delegated to them.

PANCHAYATI RAJ INSTITUTIONS

Do's

- Take the responsibility *suo motu* to help people solve their problems locally.
- Facilitate local solutions to developmental problems by bringing together of the relevant factors.
- Focus on developmental as well as non-developmental functions.
- Improve service delivery. Encourage people's participation in all services.
- Give special importance to governance, especially in providing citizen entitlement properly and in grievance redressal.
- Hold stakeholder consultation periodically.
- Improve the quality of participation, particularly in gram sabhas and other fora.
- Devote considerable energy to local resource mobilisation through tax, user charges, contributions, voluntary work, etc.
- Have a clear perspective development plan for creation of infrastructure, natural resource management, increase of production, job generation, etc.
- Build up a data base required for planning and validate it through participation.
- Ensure transparency of all dealings.
- Follow the due process while taking decision on resource allocations in selecting beneficiaries.
- Keep all the registers up-to-date and prepare the accounts according to schedule.
- Make concerted efforts to include the excluded groups in the development process.
- Publish a Citizen's Charter dealing with the level of services which the Panchayat is willing to guarantee to the citizen.
- Introduce participatory monitoring systems. Voluntarily subject all actions to social audit.

Don'ts

- Don't look up to the State Government for everything.
- Don't be clones of the State Government's Department in behaviour or in practice.
- Don't bring in divisive party politics in matters related to Panchayat functioning.
- Avoid patronage while taking decisions.
- Don't focus on distribution of benefits.
- Don't stifle diversity.
- Don't go in for costly technologies and solutions while dealing with local development problems.

3

From Representation to Presence

The Paradox of Power and Powerlessness

Kumud Sharma

I

Advocacy for democratic decentralisation has been part of the liberal democratic tradition. The value of decentralisation is well argued as it is expected to provide greater efficiency, transparency, accountability, responsiveness and opportunities for people's participation. Decentralisation is also advocated due to economic complexities and socio-cultural diversities and the need for the state to pay attention and respond to the diverse needs of the region and social groups who demand 'voice from below' and reject uniformities. The notion of plurality and diversity, based on class, caste, ethnicity, religion and gender, which is central to liberal democracy, also reflects problems of inclusion and exclusion, and unequal citizenship rights, and demand for political representation is seen as a legitimate means of protecting interests of socially disadvantaged groups. The demand for political inclusion of groups, which we see themselves as marginalised, excluded or silenced, is at the heart of demand for political representation.

Theorists and critics of liberal democracy question the homogenising presumptions of the concept of 'common good' or a 'common purpose' in plural societies, as there are multiplicity of arenas within which power is exercised and there are vital links between one set of people's struggles and another, particularly for those more concerned with 'human agency' and a minimum level of capabilities that ensure a degree of participation. There is a need to go beyond the liberal democratic formulation of the notions of gender equality.

The interest group's politics demanding representation in elected bodies on the basis of class, ethnic, religion and gender identities has been interpreted as a shift from the 'politics of ideas' to 'politics of presence' (Philips, 1998). The 'politics of presence' foregrounds the question as to who represents whom? 'Politics of presence' implies something other than pursuing party politics and their agendas as it is argued that our "interests are better protected if we are represented by those who share our experiences and interests" (J. Burnheim, 1985). More than 200 years back, a group of French women stated, "Just as a nobleman cannot represent a plebian and the latter cannot represent a nobleman, so a man, no matter how honest he may be, cannot represent, a woman. Between the representatives and the represented, there must be an absolute identity of interests" (a group of French Women in 1789; cited in Anne Philips, 1998).

Women's movement's demand for reservation was based on shared ideals and goals of political representation was seen as an instrument for social and economic transformation.

> "a political system cannot be based on ideology alone but must keep in touch with the actualities of the social situation...The continuing under-representation of women prevents their proper participation in the decision making process in the country...When one applies the principles of democracy to a society characterised by tremendous inequalities, such special protections are only spearheads to pierce through the barriers of inequality. An unattainable goal is as meaningless as a right that cannot be exercised" (CSWI, 1975).

While it is difficult to empirically test the validity of the notion of shared experiences, shared beliefs and goals as a precondition for interest group representation as it hides multiplicity of identities, interests and experiences of women behind such universalism, however, there is a definite need to see the links between representation, participation and deliberative democracy. The arguments for fair representation of women or quotas derive its legitimacy from the 'politics of ideas'. The opposition to the idea of reservation comes from those who emphasise other identities (caste, community, etc.) against the identity of an essentialist category 'women'.

Issues of women's representation being debated in the 90s not only raise a set of questions about citizenship, women's rights and feminist politics, but clearly demonstrate how social and economic inequalities combined with cultural values make it harder for women to challenge dominant ideologies and structures (Sharma, 2001).

The problem of political equality and equal participation, however, depends on more fundamental changes in social, economic and educational conditions. The deceptive simplicity of the notion of 'political equality' hides overt and covert forms of gender discriminations and the political reflection of these in levels of participation and influence. The preoccupation with state interventions tends to ignore the power relations that underpin decision-making processes. Numerous political analysts have deliberated upon the disturbing correlation between social class and levels of participation and representation and gender.

Many of the arguments for women's equal participation move within well-defined territories inherited from the practices of liberal democracy. The demand for political representation by women has, however, significantly altered the political terrain...Besides being contentious, it has become one of the many avenues for challenging existing hierarchies of power. Women argue that greater representation is needed to influence the redistribution of power and resources, redefine political agendas and articulate women's interests and critical questions of distribution of power. Democracy does not mean paternalism. It is obvious that women have begun to understand ways in which power is shared and exercised and why demand for greater representation is seen not only as a means to redress gender imbalance in formal politics but also as an instrument for redistribution of power and resources.

The philosophical question of self-governance, access to power by disadvantaged sections in society and problems faced by women have to be located within wider debates on politics, society, economy and culture. Society should not only compensate women for past injustice but should also eliminate socio-cultural and legal impediments to women's equal participation. Political representation is not a goal in itself as the broader understanding of the processes of political structures and power, the ideology of state, the interrelationship between class, caste and gender is important. Those arguing for affirmative action believe that 'institutionalised inequalities' need institutionalised counter-measures (Mazumdar, 1997). Others argue that 'reservations are not a matter of principle... they are at best a limited intervention in a larger repertoire of affirmative action strategies designed in specific context' (Singh, 1997).

Political participation is an exercise in power. Two sets of issues affect women's participation – the first relates to the nature of representative democracy and the second relates to the status of political equality and citizenship. Women have to grapple with both the issues of representation and governance and the nature of politics and political institutions in a multi-party democratic system. Democratic politics has increasingly focused attention on the composition and behaviour of existing elites and the limits of representative democracy. Coalition politics in India has demonstrated its own contradictions, which cannot always accommodate legitimate concern in its political agenda because of its survival concerns.

Underrepresentation of women in politics is an empirical fact. However, efficacy of representation will depend on a range of enabling conditions – political context, vigorous advocacy on behalf of women, choice of mechanisms and its likely outcomes, proceduralism or how the terms of participation get determined and the need to address exclusions inherent in the political parties' packaging of ideas and the contested terrain of politics and enforced choices and preferences.

The demand for 'political presence' is also now reformulated in terms of fairness and social justice. The relationship between democracy and justice is perennially troubled. Arguments for social and gender justice are inappropriate if they proceed in isolation from the existing institutional arrangements or if we believe that no more initiatives are needed on normative principles that regulate relationship between different social groups. When policies are worked out without involving hitherto politically excluded groups, they are unlikely to engage with these concerns.

Those arguing for political representation or gender parity in representation believe that there is a case for a 'threshold level' or a 'critical mass' that ensures that women's concerns will be adequately addressed. In 1988, Drude Dahlerup in her study on the relevance of the concept of 'critical mass' in Scandinavian politics established a threshold of 30-33 per cent women start influencing the institutions. The political engagement of women can change initial preferences and can help in formulating new positions. It anticipates the introduction of new concerns and interests and a process in which these will generate a wider range of policy considerations. The argument for changing the gender composition of elected bodies is compelling as it rests on several possibilities which might emerge rather than on certainties of changing the political structures and agendas. While the issue of affirmative action is on the political agenda, the pressure of party politics and the ambiguity over how far gender quotas can accommodate the determined pursuit of women's interests, remain contentious.

II
HOW HAVE WOMEN'S ISSUES IN PRIs CONCEPTUALISED AND ARTICULATED?

More general literature on Women and PRIs has a preoccupation with certain structural problems that women face rather than issues of gender ideology and social and cultural dynamics. There are two traditions of intellectual inquiry on women in local self-government – the one, which sees local governance reforms such as bringing functional, financial and administrative autonomy and accountability, efficiency and effectiveness of these institutions as a prerequisite for bottom up approach to planning, while the other approach emphasises the gendering of the institutions of local self-government and the political nature of the issue. Apparently, there has been some political posturing and lip sympathy to people-centred and participatory democracy. However, the deradicalised agenda of PRIs sidetracks several of the ideological issues. There seems to be growing polarisation between the ideologies of local self-government and the questions of devolution of power. The changing dynamics of power relationship in a multi-party democratic system generates its own counter pulls and pressures. Buch argues that the 'two axes of development and governance' are not irreconcilable, yet the democratic institution *vs.* the anxiety about development has almost invariably led to an instrumentalist approach in looking at Panchayats... The vagueness about the main objectives of such bodies — participation or efficiency, empowerment or cost effectiveness, good governance, more development, power to local people to participate in governance or only effective delivery of services - add to the confusion. Are these goals really irreconcilable?

The insights gained from empirical studies clearly indicate :

- The gap between the radical and the real, and the overall attitude of political leadership and bureaucracy towards these changes;
- The Panchayat leadership and access to power to weaker sections in society;
- The politico-administrative aspects and the practical problems of finance, administration, governance and development. The District Planning Committees have replaced the earlier District Planning and Development Councils. However, the economic plans are still prepared by the officers of the concerned departments;
- Problems with power sharing arrangements between states and PRIs; and
- The gap between the notion of social and gender justice and the strategies for empowering women.

The chapter addresses the last question of opportunities for women's participation in deliberative as well as decision-making processes of PRIs. Most of the studies have pointed out that the problems faced by elected women representatives are due to illiteracy, lack of any formal knowledge of procedures or statecraft, resistance from male dominated political and bureaucratic structures, existing traditional rural, social and political environment. There is also a feeling among some sections that reservation is a principle imposed from above and is not going to change traditional mindsets, dominance and interference by male members, non-cooperation by bureaucracy or obstacles put by influential political leaders. Women do have limited direct access to political leadership at higher levels which is reflected in their work, confidence and influence. The elected representatives have been constitutionally equipped with many powers. However, most of them have no knowledge of such powers and they fail to exercise themselves or it is surrogately exercised by others. Improving the participation of a group through quotas within traditionally defined spheres of politics may be according to some misdirected though it has the potential as one of the strategies in 'a radical politics of subversion' (Menon, 2000).

Empirical studies include both 'narratives of courage' and 'narratives of dislocations' that disrupt the presumed outcomes of women's political representation in PRIs.

A field study in five districts of Madhya Pradesh (1994) selected 94 women Sarpanchs out of a total of 188 belonging to scheduled castes from the districts of Ujjain, Dewas, Ratlam, Shajapur and Mandsuar. In the first election in MP, the study points out that women elected were from the families which were the opinion makers and continued to play the role from behind the scene. Scheduled caste members face both male domination and caste domination.

Not all the women have volunteered to contest the election but have been motivated by a number of organisations, individuals and institutions. The women representatives who were active in NGOs/political groups in the area were depending more on the opinion leaders of the village. The of recruitment, caste, party affiliation, family and organisational affiliation, peer group, own reputation and past services to the community. G. Palanithurai categorises women leaders as those propelled by the male members of their families; those oriented by NGOs, by the parties or motivated by the community; and those sponsored by their husbands with the support of political party (Palanithurai, 2000).

A report from UP states that "women were catapulted into positions of leadership at all levels of the panchayat structure. Given the prevailing social conditions in the state, a large number of women chairpersons (and members) are merely proxies of menfolk...In the famous Amethi Parliamentary Constituency from where Rajiv Gandhi – the architect of the 73rd Amendment and 1/3rd reservation of seats for women– contested election to the Lok Sabha; a study of the Gram Sabhas (143) indicates that the ones which are headed by women Pradhans are in the worst situation as the function of Pradhans are under 'double jeopardy'. Women representatives face an insurmountable barriers in the form of gender-insensitive bureaucracy which finds it easier to align itself with rural male elites." (Sahbhagi Shikshan Kendra, Lucknow). Some brave women have succeeded in breaking the barriers. In Punjab and Haryana, economic development goes hand in hand with strong biases against women.

Strategies adopted by men to prevent women from contesting elections can take more subtle forms i.e. using traditional family values and structures to break women's resolve to enter the political space, using sons and husbands to get her to withdraw nomination papers, or even subject her to violence if she refuses to bend down under such pressures and patriarchal bargains. For the poor and landless women workers depending for their survival on those who control productive assets, the threats to their survival and livelihoods act as major structural constraints (Stephens, 2001).

The CWDS' study of Panchayats and women in the states of Uttar Pradesh, Rajasthan and Madhya Pradesh, completed in 1999, sought to examine the processes of women's representation and participation; their experiences, problems, support, copying mechanisms and the linkage between their political, economic, social and overall empowerment. The study counters four myths about women's entry into PRIs and their likely performance, i.e., passivity and disinterest in entering political institutions; only upper caste/class women will benefit from reservation; importance of their political connections and women mostly being proxy candidates. The study noted increased aspirations and confidence levels and lack of understanding of the potential for alliance building between different collectives of rural women which continue to work in a compartmentalised manner with separate agendas (Buch, 1999).

Apparently, the studies entail a range of ambivalent constructions which are open-ended and contested. It would be naïve to believe that giving women representation in PRIs would address issues of social and gender justice. There is a difference between women who come from families with political background and those termed as 'first generation political aspirants'. Enabling women's participation through reservation is an important step but more fundamental changes are needed of democratic practices and institutions.

The dimensions on mediating frameworks and strategies have laid emphasis on training and advocacy to deepen the movement for democratic decentralisation.

Training Intervention as a Strategy

During the last nine years of Panchayati Raj, there has been a strong argument to mobilise, train, inform and equip women in leadership skills and strengthen their understanding of the processes that enhance their abilities to claim their due share of power and resources. Several issues have emerged out of the processes involving training interventions.

Training programmes are vital to enable women to understand their roles but such programmes should ensure continuity and touch upon several aspects not only on the basics of Panchayati Raj and knowledge about government schemes. The government training programmes lack a comprehensive and gender sensitive approach. The NGOs' training programmes are limited in terms of outreach and frequency, though strong on ideological front. Women face multiple oppressions and have to cope with additional problems of domestic responsibilities, travel expenses, patriarchal control on their mobility. The training package has to be more meaningful which imparts practical skills and encourages them to take on the political challenge.

Lack of empathy and support to PRIs by political and bureaucratic structures has created innumerable hurdles in the functioning of these agencies. Attempts at capacity building of elected women representatives get sabotaged by institutionalised inequalities and pressures.

Voluminous literature on training intervention has emphasised that training methods have to be contextual, comprehensible, interactive, adaptive and participatory. The areas which have received maximum attention are – training framework and approaches, capacity building of training institutions, preparation of training material (ideological and practical content) and networking among training institutions. The Rajiv Gandhi Foundation Task Force on 'Training Intervention' underscored the importance of gender sensitisation as it cuts across all kinds of oppression and subjugation. Emphasising that there is a need for making these provisions truly effective which would require empowering women and doing away with surrogate representatives, it pointed out that "training of women representatives must not begin with the promise that women are themselves responsible for the lack of social and cultural capital. The situation is a systematic failure. Therefore, even the trainer must start from what the participants know and then take them to the arena of the unknown...Building up community support networks for women members should be an important component of training intervention" (RGF Task Force Report, 2001).

Murthy (1998) distinguishes between five different approaches to what she calls 'gender transformative capacity building' i.e. the conceptual approach, the policy analysis approach, the empirical approach, the action-reflected approach and the experiential approach. Very few analytical studies are available to demonstrate what methodologies have worked in different contexts.

A review of a training exercise (Stephen, 2001) covering about 11,000 women in eight districts of Karnataka, over a four years' period, noted interesting transformations in women after the third and fourth phases in training. There were also instances of women abandoning the fight halfway due to lack of support from their husbands and other village people. A pilot study, with 60 G.P. members, who had undergone a three-phased training, revealed that one-third were functioning as proxy candidates, one-third did not face any constraints at home but found it difficult to overcome gender subordination within the Gram Panchayat and about one-third were functioning effectively and have gained some power within the family. Stephen argues that the debate between trainers and activists on training strategies (empowerment strategies and mobilisation *vs.* structured learning process within specific time-frame) is valid and the interface between the two is critical and not mutually exclusive. Training should ultimately lead to institutional changes and renegotiation of socially and culturally constructed boundaries.

While desirability of an effective and ideologically grounded training programme cannot be over-emphasised, the importance of the macro-economic and social dynamics and larger political environment cannot be ignored. Emphasis on procedures and programmes, rather than political process and critical issues that women have to confront, is not going to qualitatively change the participation of women. Majority of women representatives are now showing their determination to occupy public space and are fighting for their rights and the legitimate spaces. In their struggle against entrenched systems disempowering them, they have to overcome many hurdles such as conditions of poverty, social responsibility for the domestic unit, growing criminalisation of political process and interlocking of other social relations with gender relations. Some of these issues are discussed below.

Patriarchies of State, Political Parties and Communities

The language of state politics, procedures of political parties for recruitment and nomination and political socialisation of men and women reflect conflictual relationship between women's representation and political leadership. Most of the political parties remain institutionalised sites of patriarchal power (despite some ruling matriarchs). Women are expected to adjust to the imperatives of party structures for political survival and often get co-opted in the process, rather than influencing party structures and processes. The more rigid the party structures are the more alienating women members find it to be. A study from Kerala points out that "male party bosses did not favour the emergence of independent women who revealed a degree of feminist consciousness. The political parties saw them as not amenable to control and considered them as liabilities". It further states that "most of the women, who contested the last Panchayat election, were not politically rooted in their own right... Those who manifested a degree of independence and had been involved earlier in women's activism along non-party lines, were effectively excluded both by the Left and the Congress-led fronts" (Chathukulam and John, 2001).

The model state of Kerala where the scale and magnitude of the decentralisation process and transferring of powers, function and resources is considered to be the most significant achievement of the state combined with a viable and realistic planning from below. A study based on extensive interviews of 27 women members claims that women representatives have not been able to change the style and practice of the wider political arena. Commenting on the People's Plan Campaign in Kerala, the study concludes that the participatory plan campaigns were gender insensitive as women were not involved in participatory exercises (data collection, preparation of development report as it needed late working hours). Resource persons of the campaign were predominantly male (only 8 per cent women) and only ten per cent women were members of the block level expert communities, which appraised the projects. The organisational structure of the plan campaign was totally male dominated as the support organisation (KSSP) is overwhelmingly dominated by men (Chathukulam and John, 2001). This happens in a state where literacy is not such a big problem.

Selection of beneficiaries for anti-poverty programme, implementation of development projects, policy decisions on resources and other priorities remain contentious areas due to conflicting interests between party bosses, planning boards and women representatives. Some of the problems are part of the changing scenario and need adjustments on the part of both traditional power structures as well as the emerging ones with new entrants.

The problems get further complicated when one relocates these questions within a more complex matrix of identity politics. Caste, religious and ethnic identities have often prevailed over gender identity. Women who come in under caste reservations have come in with their social and economic disadvantages, poverty, illiteracy and dependence on wage labour (Vyasulu and Vyasulu, 1999). The questions of caste and the discourse on 'social justice' in the public-political domain, growing presence of backward castes, demand for political representation of communities and the agenda for 'gender justice' challenging the gendered *status quo* within political system have posed a challenge to the state.

The state with its slogan of 'empowerment of women' and its restricted meaning with haphazard way of addressing systemic problems has hardly made a dent in institutions shaping development policies and agenda. The over-proliferation and contradictions in policy pronouncements often lead to non-implementation, poor performance or silent withdrawals.

The Constitutional Amendment has a transformative potential and women have reported new recognition and respect from their families and communities in statements such as "they call me member *saab*" or "they offer me a chair" or it is a matter of pride for *dalit* women when upper caste men come to her with respects. The family support comes from those families which had not shared power in traditional rural social structures and see women elected representatives bringing prestige to the family (Buch, 1999; Tekchandani *et. al.*, 1997).

These profiles of assertion, participation and courage continue to co-exist with widespread belief in women's passivity, ignorance, male interference and women as proxies as Panchayats also replicate the rural power structures (Leiten, 1996; Sudha Pai, 1998; Mishra, Kumar and Pal, 1997). Resistance to women continues and sometimes there is a backlash and even physical violence. There have been sustained efforts to unseat them through no confidence motions.

Misuse of No Confidence Motion

This has become yet another method by which women Sarpanchs are prevented from completing their terms in office. Sarkar notes that while there are rules as to how a no confidence motion must be handled (who will preside, whom notice has to be sent, etc.), there is no requirement that the reasons for asking for a no-confidence motion be given. Men are even today reluctant to accept women as an equal (Sarkar, 2001). Buch also reports that in Madhya Pradesh, Chairpersons elected in 1994 elections in three district panchayats had to face legal battles. In one of the cases, despite winning in successive court battles, her position is continued to be occupied by the male vice-chairperson. Another method of targeting women in Madhya Pradesh is the use of 'right to recall' elected Panchayat and municipal presidents. After the amendment, two presidents – both women – had to face the ordeal (Buch, 2001).

NGOs working in Gujarat have found elected women to be easy victims of the no-confidence motion. No woman was elected to the position of vice-president. Male vice-presidents did not cooperate with the women presidents making it difficult for them to perform the functions properly. This in turn led to a no-confidence motion against her. If a woman is strong and honest while performing her duties, the male colleagues see her as a threat and try and manipulate a no-confidence motion against her (Ramesh and Ali, 2001).

The plight of scheduled caste women heading a Panchayat is even worse as they suffer from 'double jeopardy' i.e. patriarchy as well as the casteist attitudes.

Problems of Mandatory Rotation of Reserved Seats

Most of the studies have found that the five years' term is not adequate to adjust to new roles and responsibilities and learn the ropes. Unfulfilled expectations of their constituencies and political inexperience lead to frustration. The experience gained by women members is low as many of them may not like to or may be discouraged to contest from general constituencies. It may be total loss to public life unless parties recognise the experience gained by them.

Several studies report that a majority of women would not like to contest in the next round of elections. Is this an indication of women's inability to cope with multiple demands and pressures or is it due to great deal of opposition from local politicians and rural elites?

In some states, in case of chairperson's office, the reservation is for a shorter duration and is resented by many people. Instances of violence, no-confidence motions and other forms of harassment are noted in several studies (Buch, 1999). She noted that 'the rotation system has a disempowering effect as there is a constant effort to downgrade their performance and discouraging them from being effective'. She suggests the creation of multi-member constituency as a way out of this dilemma.

Gram Sabha and the Issue of a Sub-Quorum of Women within the General Quorum

The importance of Gram Sabha in the Panchayati Raj system has been emphasised. However, it has yet to take root. Poor attendance, particularly of women and poorer sections, problems of quorum and procedures adopted for finalising development plans and projects have created a general attitude of skepticism towards Gram Sabhas as an effective instrument of participatory local government. It is one thing to argue that

Gram Sabha should serve as a forum for discussing developmental issues with active participation from different sections. If Gram Sabhas are not to become a forum for legitimising decisions taken by elites than the issue of quality of participation needs to be taken up seriously. The question of timings of such meetings, settlement patterns of villages and long distances to be trekked, quality of deliberations and manipulation of discussions by dominant groups, have important consequences for Gram Sabha meetings.

Disqualification of Elected Representatives on the Basis of Number of Children

This provision is gender-neutral but its implications are not. The RGF Study (1998) mentions that the inclusion of this clause has proved somewhat significant as by March, 1998. Four hundred seventeen Ward Panchs, 38 Sarpanchs and 5 members of Panchayat Samitis had been disqualified.

Through a writ petition in the Rajasthan High Court, 12 elected Panches challenged the order in terms of the legality of the orders of the Chief Executive Officer and to his jurisdiction to hold an inquiry in the matter. While the High Court rejected the petition and sustained the state's legislative competence to make such a law, it acknowledged that "having more than two children does not in any way affect the working of the Sarpanch and upheld the validity of such a provision on the ground that 'these provisions' have been enacted by the legislature to control the menace of population explosion..."

Similar petitions filed before the High Court of Punjab and Haryana raised an additional point that 'the two child norm goes against the personal laws as some of the petitioners were Muslims'. The High Court while rejecting the petitions opined that 'the legislature has rightly come forward by imposing reasonable restrictions in the interest of the State...how can one expect the citizens of this country to live with human dignity and social equality when the population goes on increasing by leaps and bounds' (cited in Sarkar, 2001). A similar disqualification clause does not exist for elected members at state and national levels. Linking up population control programmes with the democratisation of local governance raise doubts about state's seriousness in seeing women play an active role in institutions of local self-government. Women's organisations call it an attempt to dilute and subvert the spirit of the 73rd and 74th Amendments.

The concepts of rights and justice are not mere abstractions but provide the ideological basis for some degree of vibrancy in social and political dynamics. In the Indian context, the search for alternative strategies for women's development/ empowerment with a new emphasis on gender or social justice include a reexamination of basic concepts of democracy, development, citizenship, representation and participation as well as an understanding of structures of gender inequalities and imbalances. The ability of women to participate in democratic processes and institution building is greatly influenced by pressures from women's grassroots initiatives and movements. The transformation impact may vary across regions. However, there is incontestable evidence of grassroots organisation's role in supporting, influencing and resisting statist development agenda, social and cultural barriers, male resistance and strengthen women's participation.

Women's Grassroots Initiatives and the Transformation of the Public Sphere

Politics is about participation in public sphere but for women's movement both the personal and the public domain are equally political as fluid boundaries separate the public and the private domain. The simplistic appeals for women's equal political participation leave out some of the difficult questions unanswered, e.g. institutional arrangements and diverse patriarchal forces which condition women's choices, ambition and ability to represent women politically. A more nuanced understanding of gender issues is needed to explain not only factors that undermine women's capacities but also explore texts of resistance and opening of new spaces through women's community level activism.

The demand for reservation had its origin in decades of campaigns and protests by women's movement raising some fundamental questions about the nature of politics and democracy and emphasis on grassroots activism and participation. If women's representation does not provide space to introduce new interests and concerns then their inclusion becomes only symbolic. Despite the fact that the state has appropriated the discourse on women's empowerment, the political commitment to struggle for women's rights is marginal to the state agenda. To construct a discursive model of public sphere with openness to issues of gender inequality and difference is important. One can think of further initiatives to strengthen women's role in politics through use of open forums, linking women representatives to activists from women's movement and new mechanisms of consultations and support at community level.

The rich experience of grassroots organisations of women demonstrates that they do provide a support base to women from marginalised communities as they gain a new identity. Intermediary organisations and NGOs have also contributed to the process of transformation through advocacy and capacity building strategies. The practical experiences of grassroots organisations suggest multiple strategies and approaches to realigning power relationships. Organising women for political empowerment calls for experimentations with alternative organisation forms to create spaces and use these spaces for more transformative agenda.

References

Begin, Monique (1998): Towards a Critical Mass: Women in Politics, J. P. Naik Memorial Lecture, Centre for Women's Development Studies, New Delhi.

Buch, N. (1999): From Oppression to Assertion : A Study of Panchayats and Women in Madhya Pradesh, Rajasthan and Uttar Pradesh, CWDS (Mimeo), New Delhi.

Burnheim, J. (1985): *Democracy Possible?* Cambridge.

Chathukulam, Jos and M.S. John (2000): Empowerment of Women Panchayat Members : Learning from Kerala (India) in *Asian Journal of Women's Studies*, Vol. 6, No. 4.

Gender and Governance : A Country Paper, Center for Women's Development Studies, New Delhi (forthcoming).

Gender Issues in Panchayats in Uttar Pradesh : A Report by Sahbhagi Kendra, Lucknow

Leiten, G.K. (1996): Panchayats in Western Uttar Pradesh 'Namesake Members', *Economic and Political Weekly*, Vol. 31, No. 39.

Mazumdar, Vina, (1997): Historical Soundings, *Seminar*, 457, September, Delhi.

Meena, T.R. *Panchayati Raj: Prevalent Situation – A Case Study of Kerala.*

Palanithurai, G. (2000): Status of Women Leaders in Local Bodies: Experience from Tamil Nadu. Paper presented at the *Seminar on Women in Local Governance: Experiences and Effective Intervention Strategies in Karnataka, Kerala, Andhra Pradesh, Tamil Nadu and Maharashtra,* organised by ISST, Bangalore.

Phillips, Anne (1995): Dealing with Difference : A Politics of Ideas or a Politics of Presence? In *Democracy and Difference : Contesting the Boundaries of the Political* (ed.) Seyla Benhabib, Princeton University Press, Princeton, NJ.

Ramesh, Asha and Bharati Ali (2001; 33.3): Reservation Towards Political Empowerment, *Books for Change*, Bangalore.

Sarkar, Lotika (1997-98): *Annual Survey of Indian Law*, Vol. xxxiii-iv, The Indian Law Institute, New Delhi.

Sharma, Kumud (1998): Transformative Politics : Dimensions of Women's Participation in Panchayati Raj, *Indian Journal of Gender Studies*, Vol. 5(1), Sage Publications, Delhi.

Stephen, F. (2001): Empowering Women in Panchayats through Training, in *Building Women's Capacities : Interventions in Gender Transformations* (ed.) Ranjini K. Murthy, Sage Publications India Pvt. Ltd., New Delhi.

Tekchandani, Bharati, Jyoti Kiran and Priti Sharma (eds.). *They Call Me Member Saab: Women in Haryana Panchayati Raj*, MARG, New Delhi.

The Problem – Empowering Women : A Symposium on Political Reservations for Women, in *Seminar*, 457, September 1997, Delhi.

Vyasulu, Poornima and Vinod Vyasulu (1999): Women in Panchayati Raj: Grassroots Democracy in Malgudi, *Economic and Political Weekly*, December 25.

Papers/Reports sent by RGF.

Women in Panchayati Raj: Gender Perspective: A Report from Mahatma Gandhi State Institute of Rural Development, Jabalpur, (M.P.)

4

Emerging Institutions for Rural Development

Yoginder K. Alagh

Introduction

Somehow the atmosphere has been created that globalisation and corporatisation are the only sustainable ways of developing rural India. I genuinely believe that Indian agriculture is peasant based. Markets are very powerful way of supporting atomistic peasant based institutions. But community organisations and limited and focused cooperative forms of institutions are critical at the present phase of development. They are not a part of the central policy debates, because these are set by thinktanks with little roots in India and the debate on sustainable development policy with alternative mindsets does not seem to have a market in official policy making institutions, abroad and at home. But that does not mean that the alternative theories do not explain developments or have application possibilities. In the world of ideas, turnarounds anyway take place in ways we do not understand. I show in this lecture that a number of the arguments used in dominant thinking are irrelevant. Community-based institutions with a sharp focus will have to be central to the next phase of rural development policies in India. Profitability rates have gone down in the agricultural sector in the period of liberalisation. Instead of critically examining the causes, the argument still continues, on the old lines. There is no thinking by finance, planning and central bank policy makers on meshing strategic developmental policy rules with market reform; and so the faster the deterioration the more shrill the repetition. Now the trade debate and its meshing with sustainable development possibilities is also getting priority. India's Aggregate Measure of Support is probably no longer negative, but to some there is no change in the argument. Fortunately responding to some of us, our international negotiators have taken a more sensible position. But the changes needed at home are still not sharply defined. I have argued in my Gandhi Smruti lectures that this centering of the debate with arguments outside India is at best insufficient and at worse immoral (Alagh in Gangrade and Radhakrishna, 2000). But my purpose here is to argue that alternative possibilities are not only possible, but even global experience suggests that there are better ways of organising rural India, so that it can unleash its own creative energies (For example see the documentation at the expert level for the UN Secretary General's Millennium Conference : See Y.K. Alagh, Keynote Address on Development and Governance, in Van Ginkel and Thakur, UNU Millennium Series, 2001 pp. 73-82). My objective is to encourage a debate, since my own thinking is at a formative stage and also at Ahmedabad, in the rural taluka of Dascroi I have more time to think. Also this is the least we can do in the cause of sustainable development.

The Problems

We explore three critical areas. First, how can communities and individuals in fragile regions and at risk, turn around? In other words, how can sustainable development strategies be operationalised? The institutional question here is the socio-economic rules and incentives and disincentives, so that organisations and structures are in position to foster replicability of success stories. Second, what are the policy and macro implications of supporting these strategies? Here the period of 'globalisation'. After the East Asian crisis, the Washington Consensus is being superimposed with this (is giving up to?), in many countries, (See Jomo, K.S., 2000 for the growth and distribution impacts of the East Asian crisis) although the new strand of reasoning has little impact on India. In fact until 1999/2000, even the Economic Survey had little discussion of the East Asian meltdown. Development strategies are by definition mobilisational in the sense of resource raising, but do we have the wisdom to develop systems which will genuinely help those who help themselves, or will resources, technology and organisation support always and only, be a part of commerce, the urge of dominance and double speak. Here, even the blue prints are vague. At least the rules of structural adjustment were clear – "abolish controls, reduce government, reduce tariffs and never have special policies for employment or development of backward areas". The rules of helping those who help themselves are not known. The power of modern technology and decentralised markets is known. But how do we use this power for areas where markets and resource backups are weak, is not quite clear. What are some of the areas where development concerns will need structures at the regional, national and global levels? Third and finally, can partnerships be talked about if the language of the other is not known. What are the requirements of participation and transparency? How can they be made a part of functioning systems? This is a question of alternate thinking styles at which India was very good at one stage, but alas no more. However, the least we should do is to borrow sensibly from experience elsewhere.

Sustainable Livelihood for the Marginalised

Consistent agricultural growth over a period has led to decline in rural poverty levels in the areas where such growth takes place. The so-called Green Revolution areas are a case in point. Agricultural growth of 3.5 per cent annual plus for two decades or so invariably led to critical elimination of hunger and significant declines in poverty levels. But such growth took place in areas with good soil and assured rainfall or irrigation supplies. FAO studies showed that the elasticity of cropping intensively with respect to irrigation was around 0.3 and so assured water supply was land augmenting and of land productivity with respect to irrigation was above 0.5 (See Agriculture Towards 2010). As the Japanese economist Y. Hayami has shown (1981), this kind of growth raised the demand for labour, employment went up and poverty levels declined. The model of atomistic peasant agriculture worked here. The benefits of state supported agricultural research could reach the farmer, provided land rights were established. Input and output disposal markets, worked since irrigation technology and market support were very much, a part of this strategy, it worked in selected areas.

Planning work in India, for example, worked it (See Alagh, 1988, 1989, 1990 and Planning Commission, 1989). In the early eighties, the critics called it the favoured crop, favoured region model. Another critic described the planning of this strategy as limited and linear thinking. The problem, however, was in areas where these initial favourable conditions did not exist. They were bypassed in the growth process. In India, in the first phase of the Green Revolution, in a fifth of the districts growth was negative and in another two fifths it couldn't keep up with population growth levels. In Sahelian Africa, many countries in the rest of Africa and in some countries in Latin America, the situation was worse and continued to remain so. The prime issue of institutional development and policy is to reverse this process. With all the advances made in an understanding of both the organisation of agriculture, technology and resource management, persistence of mass poverty and hunger is a striking contrast to claims of universal progress.

An interesting aspect of these problems is its relationship with environmental problems. These are "fragile eco-regions". They are the arid and semi-arid regions described in the FAO-UNESCO agro-economic atlas of the World (See Alexandratos, 1993). They are the hill slopes with declining tree cover and rainfall causing soil erosion. They are the coastal areas with mangroves disappearing. They are the saline lands and the problematic soils. These are, as in the plateaux and arid regions in India, areas in which through time, communities had established a balance between carrying capacity and human need. There was poverty, but also time honoured practices of sustaining the fragile resource base with activities, technologies and customs which had evolved through centuries of experimentation and adoption. In the last century, dramatic reductions in mortality and resource demands from outside had rudely shaken the carrying capacity balance of such areas.

In the preparation for the Rio Conference and particularly at the Hague Symposium and Declaration, some of us had argued that the problems of the global commons cannot be meaningfully negotiated without addressing this problem. Sea warming, global warming and the biodiversity questions cannot be addressed through global negotiations, if local communities are out of balance with their land and water resources. This was articulated in the Hague Declaration of which I was a signatory and for which I had worked and was drafted by Mahabub-ul-Haq and J. Pronk (See 1992). These ideas were ultimately reflected in the Rio Declaration and Agenda 21.

Very little organised work is available on successful models under these conditions. In the late eighties, in India, an attempt was made to build up a set of best practice cases, which had worked. I had summarised them in work done for starting an agro-climatic policy exercise by the Planning Commission and in a book written for WIDER (Alagh, 1991). The cases had some common characteristics. The economic rates of return to investment were high – 18 per cent plus on the investment made. Substantial food and energy deficits of the rural communities studied were met. The technology consisted of land and water development, followed by the introduction of appropriate "cropping" sequences. On the hill slope, it was watershed development, contour building, gully plugging, work along the ridge contours. In coastal areas, it was aquifer management. In saline water logged soils, soil amendments and drainage. Vegetation cover was a part of the strategy. Generally, a low yielding cereal was substituted by a two-crop sequence or tree cover either of which helped to consolidate the soil further.

From the replicability angle, there were some interesting features. Leadership at the community level was important in all these cases. Generally, the leadership group had some science background. The leaders were from NGO, or social work organisations, retired army personnel, civil servants and in one case a farmer. The technology for the falling profitability can only be explained by inefficiency in the working of the market. The case for reform in the state sponsored pricing system to encourage diversification of Indian agriculture is very clear. So is the need to remove bureaucratic controls on commodity movements in India and for exports. But the effectiveness of large companies in supplying cheaper inputs in village markets of small size needs study. Their presence is necessary. Is it sufficient?

Table 4.1: Relative Price Movements in Indian Agriculture

Year	*Price Index Purchased*	*Intermediate Consumption All Commodities Sold*
1989-90	393.5	401.4
1997-98	785.4	920.1
% Increase in 97-98 over 89-90	229	199

Source: CACP, 2000, Table 4.2, p. 302

At a more basic level, the argument that since the aggregate measure of support to Indian agriculture was negative, trade liberalisation would lead to great gains to agriculture, is now revised by the Brettonwoods institutions. As compared to the Purcell-Gulati estimates of negative AMS of 28 per cent the findings for the nineties by the Purcell-Gulati studies are that the AMS is close to zero. In my arguments for the food security meeting, organised recently by the Lal Bahadur Shastri National Academy, of Administration, I showed that we were not prepared for the WTO negotiations with our mindset, for as J. Bhagwati has argued, the WTO negotiations were conducted with World Bank-IMF data bases (See Alagh, 2001). In fact, the argument now is that, given IMF definitions of government expenditure, Indian subsidies to agriculture are around 30 per cent, as compared to around a third of that level in Asian countries. The intellectual base of the present debate is indeed weak. Sharad Joshi has criticised this reasoning as Alagh Economics (Sharad Joshi, 2000). Unfortunately for us, he doesn't even understand the urgency after the East Asian meltdown as the recent work of experts like Stiglitz and R. Recupero has shown, but this debate was there all along. Ten years ago, in a WIDER monograph, I had shown that in a partially liberalising economy, efficient firms could start making losses, because the industries supplying inputs to them got more effective protection. This was the analytical base of the level playing field argument of synchronising reform in interconnected industries and phasing it to avoid negative protection to efficient producers, Lance Taylor, in his *Rocky Road to Reform* described this as a Phased Pricing Strategy (Taylor, 1991). Similar approaches are now again being suggested for the energy, agro-based and material-based industries, which have important environmental consequences.

The Planning Commission has shown in the mid-term review of the Plan that the agricultural growth rate has gone down in the nineties in a decisive manner as compared to earlier decades. This should have led to some introspection. Instead, we are being told to do more of the same, namely, let the state and community organisations withdraw. Let the process of globalisation be complete. But public investment in agriculture has gone down in a big way. Exchange control is no longer there. Public sector input supplying agencies have withered away, in areas like seeds, pesticides, credit and fertilisers. Controls on trade, investment and output are much less. Why is output growth less, then, in spite of excellent weather, and why is the agricultural investment rate going down?

A basic feature of the agricultural economy, no one is talking about is the fact that according to the detailed cost of cultivation studies analysed by the Commission on Agricultural Costs and Prices, the relative increase in input prices is much higher than in the past and is not compensated by productivity increases (See Table below). Since output prices are not rising, fast enough, agricultural profitability rates are going down (See CACP, 2000). Now this is a fairly serious matter. In the nineties, when the role of the private sector expanded very considerably in supply of seeds, agrochemicals and credit, input prices went up in a significant manner and in a relative sense. Of course, with this structure growth would go down. Also, as the Planning Commission points out, agricultural growth in backward regions has also gone down, because of a collapse of public investment. So we have both diminishing returns and cost push declines in profitability, in a period of substantial privatisation of agriculture. While the constraints on diversification in relation to domestic demand and exports can be explained by the structure of price support in India, the rise in input prices and land and water development part was generally available in the institutions in the region, although some adoptions were made locally, for example, in the saline water logged soil reclamation project. In each of the cases, the major work was at the community level. Individual landholders had to cooperate for well-defined purposes. In fragile agroecological regimes; limited cooperation is a precondition for land and water development strategies to succeed. If one farmer stays out, the contour bunds of the others will be washed out in the next monsoon. The atomistic model alone cannot work here.

The economics of these efforts led to interesting questions. While these projects had high internal rates of returns of the investments made, they ran financial losses. Generally, markets were weak in fragile regions, output prices were lower than border prices and input prices like soil amendments or water pumps higher. Also, in the initial phases, land productivity levels are lower and improve as the effort proceeds with the organic composition of the soil. Sometimes, low value productivity crops are needed to improve soil composition. While generating employment or improving access to food and energy, such activities need initial subsidies. Ignacy Sachs suggested that these be funded as "front up costs", in his summary paper for the Hague Conference. (Maurice Strong described the "two seminal meetings on environment and development ... Founex in 1971 and the Hague in 1991"). In this chapter prepared for the Rio Conference and extensively reprinted, Sachs asks for :

> "a welcome shift from crop oriented policies to production systems oriented ones, with special emphasis for the needs of small farmers". Sachs pointed out that "Alagh (1991) gives many examples of watershed development projects with a short payback period. The techniques for such projects are well-known and their impact at the level of the community would be favourable. Yet they need public funding for the front up costs. Alagh argues in favour of an agro-climatic planning in terms of alternative agricultural and farming systems in order to overcome the shortcomings of a favoured crop-region approach".

This was integrated in Agenda 21 and the Rio Conference. The effort by community level agencies is now such that in countries like India the approach is no longer at a pilot level, but is the beginning of a movement. The literature on case studies I had initiated has been extensively enlarged and a table I had presented of eight cases has been replicated for over fifty efforts (K. Chopra and G. Kadekodi, 1992). More important, the largest supported NGO in the land and water field by the EEC (Sadguru in Panchmahals) and another a group supported by a German programme (WOTER in Ahmednagar) had put under tree cover 1,24,316 acres, as verified by independent evaluations. This is just a little less than the tree cover lost in India in the years 1990-95. The EEC supported group, the advisory committee of which I chair, has recently completed a training programme for Sahelian tribal leaders supported by NORAD and the Agha Khan Foundation.

The requirements, however, are not in hundreds of thousands, but millions of hectares. Government support for such programmes in India has just about kept constant. International support has gone down. This was a period of "economic reform". Why do we find it difficult to help those who help themselves even in the core areas of local and global concern? As preparations of the Kyoto and Johannesberg meetings in show, in relation to Rio targets, and more recently, the Planning Commission in relation to a review of the current plan, we are well behind in the interrelated areas of land, water and energy.

Local, National and Global Rules

The problem of imposing a hard budget constraint at the local level and helping those who help themselves is a difficult one to address. Another way of setting the problem is to harness the great vitality of decentralised markets in replicating widespread rural growth, with institutions and organisations which foster limited and well focused areas of community and cooperative action. In fact, in the current phase even if you think of problematic seriously, you risk being called luddite. (For the ludicrous nature of the policy binds we get into See Alagh, 2001). When I was India's Energy Minister, forward looking local leaders had introduced schemes where if a village or industrial estate promised to pay the price of electricity, facilities would be provided to them urgently. I asked that national and international loan money should be accessed to such areas, since they had met the preconditions of "reform". I was told I was "islanding" proposals. I would suggest that islanding is a desirable feature, because if a community is willing to pay the price of reform, it should not be asked to wait, for the reform as designed by a global or national institution, for the system as a whole.

There is interestingly a lot of literature by political scientists, which shows that the mass of people in poor countries was not interested in the Washington Consensus kind of economic reform. Many of these studies have a very incomplete understanding of reform processes in poor countries. Islanding would mean that we would relate reform to communities and also force ourselves to work out the implications for higher order systems of such issues. This is important because the Comprehensive Development Framework should not mean setting the reform objectives from the metropolis, and bringing in safety networks later, but a genuine attempt in participative growth. For developing the structure or incentive and disincentive systems for this kind of growth, we can begin with a taxonomy of complimentarities of policy rules at different levels of policy making, like no level can spend more resources than they have access to. But resources, which are short or binding constraints at national or global levels, are elastic at local levels. For example, it is easy to buy a tax free bond of the New York civic bodies, but very little attention has been paid to markets for municipal paper in developing countries and the fiscal reform that has to precede them (See Vaidya, 1998, for a description of an exceptional effort in Ahmedabad and the difficulties faced). Watershed development, for settled agriculture alternately tree crops, reclamation of saline lands, farmers run lower level irrigation systems, aquifer management in difficult situations, like coastal aquifers, tribal irrigation cooperatives, tank irrigation have all been reported as success stories and studied. The question is replicability on a larger scale. We try to set out some rules, if applied in functioning policies may reverse the tide:

1. The success stories are community and leadership based, with leadership coming from diverse sources – a progressive farmer, an NGO, a local army retired person, a 'concerned' civil servant, a scientist working in the field. The leaders either had a science background or knew enough to adapt from a nearby science institution. The organisation structure was neither purely private ownership, nor fully community or social control. The leadership invariably argued for aggressively functioning markets and land ownership was private and agricultural operations at the household level. However, there was for land or water management, limited and well-defined cooperation. This could be drainage, soil shaping, contour management, improvement and management of lower level canals, desilting of tanks, raising embankments, fish culture, market development, controlled grazing and so on. They estimated the land and water development costs. The labour component, 'outside finance', the output in terms of food requirements met, energy requirements met and fodder supplies. There were estimates of 'economic rates of return on the

investment', i.e. at accounting border prices, with a shadow wage rate at 25 per cent higher than the market rate. Financial rates of return at market prices were also estimated. These studies showed high economic rates of return, 18 per cent plus, making them very productive investments.

2. There have to be well-identified shelfs of a large number of small projects on land, water and other infrastructure projects available for financing. It was a mistake to weaken the agroclimatic project in Western India, given the region's diversified resource base.
3. Financial institutions have to design structures such that community collateral is possible for viable projects. Such help financing groups are only one such group. Land and water development groups, local infrastructure projects, in road or communication sectors, productionising products developed in R&D institutions, training for production with improved techniques, market development schemes developed by local and community groups would be other examples.
4. Lending through a weather or project cycle would be necessary. NABARD had started a scheme of this kind in 1991 as a part of an agro-economic regionalisation strategy started by the author, gave it up in 1993 and is again starting it now (See Kapur Committee, Reserve Bank of India, 2000 for details).
5. Developing policy "champions" for sorting our administrative, financial and procedural issues at local, regional and national levels, when problems arise with these kinds of development strategies. It is reasonably certain that problems are going to arise in development experiments which are off the beaten track. The question then is: Is there somebody in the policy decision making structure who will sort out the problem? ADB reports in a detailed study of farmer managed irrigation systems that the failure cases were those where such support did not exist.

Failure here is defined as performance levels in water delivery lower than by government agencies.

Rural Diversification

Some experts say that India is not changing and is stagnating. They say that the country was changing fast in the eighties and is not doing so now. It is true that the rate of change is slower in the nineties, but the historical process of change is there and until recently, the economy was also growing fast. For example, it is no longer true that 74 per cent of the work-force depends on agriculture. In fact even in 1961, while 75.9 per cent of the work force was dependent on agriculture, only 73.5 per cent was depending on crop production. This has now gone down to 54.3 per cent, according to the National Sample Survey's 55th Round. However, we keep on saying two-thirds, sometimes three-fourths of our people depend on agriculture. There may be some change in the census numbers when they come, but that will not change the big picture. While only 54 per cent workers are engaged in crops, those in livestock, dairying, poultry and so on has doubled, from 2 per cent to 4 per cent of the workforce. As people are better off, they eat more eggs, drink more milk and eat vegetable, fruit and cheese. I showed in my Lal Bahadur Shastri Lectures (Alagh, 1992), a decade ago that as India grows faster grains grow a little more than 2 per cent annual, edible oil, sugar, cotton and milk at around 5 per cent annual and poultry and fish at 6/7 per cent plus. This has happened in the nineties and by now this diversification of the food basket is well-known. Also that it takes place at all income levels, apart from the lowest decile. However, some trends which had started in the late eighties and nineties have now deaccelerated as the following statistics show:

Sector	*% of workforce depending on sector*		
	1961	*1993/94*	*1999/2000*
Crop Production	73.5	58.1	54,3
Livestock	2.0	4.5	4.1
Forestry and Fishing	0.5	0.7	0.5

Source: NSSO and Census for 1961.

First workers depending on "logging, forestry and fishing". This was 0.5 per cent of the workforce in 1961 and is stuck at 0.5 per cent in 1999-2000. Workers in forestry have gone down, those in fishing have gone up and their combined total remains the same. Thereby hangs a tale. Demand for forestry products is going up, like everything else. In fact, we are avid readers of newspapers and demand for newsprint is exploding, also wood and all the other nice things tree crops produce, like curry patta, resins, medicinal plants and many other wonders. In the late eighties, Pant Saheb was the chairman of the PM's Advisory Board on Energy and convinced the country very correctly that even in an import control regime, forests should not be cut and wood should be freely imported. This continues, totally unnecessarily for all forest products.

The ban on logging is absolutely necessary, but the forests should be nurtured to produce everything else. This is not happening and we are becoming one of the largest importers of forest products, while many other countries are large exporters, say of medicinal plants, organic chemicals of forest origin and so on. These are all on OGL. Import duties in many cases are 10 to 15 per cent. The first thing to do is to clean up the tax system, so that forest produce, particularly what is called minor forest produce, is not discriminated against. Apple trees get protection at 60 per cent, some trees at 40 per cent but most at 10 per cent. No one knows why. The second thing is to do a market reform and let producer and joint forestry management committees enter into contracts with those who can sell. The role of cooperatives is clear. The third thing is to clean up the financing and technology support systems (See Lele, Saxena, Alagh and Mitra, 2000). Today, a tribal, who grows a tree on his own land, can't get financial accommodation for the sixth year, if he has seen the tree through five years with his own savings. Trees are not collateral. In fact, trees are a part of our religion and then the National Forest Policy, so they dare not be put a value on. If we get into the business of nurturing our forests, the sector will lead the next agricultural revolution. Poultry and dairying grew at 5 to 7 per cent annually. Forest produce demand is growing at that rate. But production growth is zero. All because of perverse policies. Now tnat we have Chhattisgarh and the North-East is planning a resource based revival I hope we will get our act together. The outlines of the required policies are clear as we have seen. We have both the technology and the market at home and abroad.

Fish is a strange story. It was growing fast at around 7 per cent annually. Local demand was growing and exports were doing well. The western region in the country was doing well in inland fishing and in the deep sea, where Maharashtra and Gujarat held sway. And then in the mid nineties it all stopped. Major projects like the FFDA were completed and no new strategies were worked out. The growth of fishermen's cooperatives stops. We do know that East Asia was our dynamic market and when they melted down one part of the fast growing market crashed out. 40 per cent of our market growing between 8 to 10 per cent stopped growing, but that should be only half the story. What happened to the other half. The inability to tap local demand was a failure. The success stories earlier were not replicated. As dairying, fish, poultry and forest produce becomes more important, knowledge about replicating success must be implemented. We must find out the answers for continued growth soon. I have deliberately talked of sectors where cooperative or well defined organisations with a base of community organisation have succeeded on a replicable scale earlier and where growth is not seen now, because I believe that reviving these branches of the economy is possible in a business like manner. These problems are complex, but it is not that modern information and knowledge systems are in compatible with them. Major thinktanks working on the character of the Neo-Fordist technological revolution, like the FAST Group of the EEC, the flexible industrial specialisation networks and others have emphasised that it is compatible strongly with networking and decentralisation. As the Science and Technology Minister of India, I had convened for UNESCO a Prepcom meeting at Bangalore for the World Science Conference at Budapest which strongly reiterated that spread of technology was an institutional and not just a technology issue. These issues need to be addressed when the largest clock manufacturer in the world located at Morbi in Saurashtra wants to relocate in China, as also the Surat diamond cutters (See Saumya Kanti Mitra, 2001).

Serious research during the last decade and a half has shown fairly conclusively that the tremendous opportunities , that are available with the new technology, require groups and systems which can manage its interdisciplinary nature, since applications cut across areas like biotechnology, communications and computerisation. If the preconditions are available, it spreads very fast, both through space and sectors of the economy and society. But if the infrastructure is not there, both physical and human, vast areas will be left out, including some in the developed world. There is also the need of quick response. As Ricardo Petralla of the EEC's FAST Group pointed out, each generation of innovations is building on the corpses of earlier ones. State and parastatal agencies find it difficult to perform in this framework. Small flexible groups responding to need work. Again, the need for partnerships, of community initiatives to back those who work is obvious. I argued with the Finance Minister that in this budget this should be one of his central tasks so that the 'Ajanta' stays home.

Much the same kind of approaches are necessary in diverse fields like education, health, urban problems, and even the debate on industrial restructuring policies. The question of synchronising and phasing reform has again gathered argument, unfortunately because he was supposed to prepare us for facing the impact of WTO agreements. The estimates he gives as Commerce Ministry, Gulati for the 88/90 period are all Purcell-Gulati estimates of the World Bank. The Bank has changed them since Purcell now works with Blairel, but we continue with our old swansong. It is also strange for Joshi to criticise me for ignoring the work of Tyagi, since it was effectively used for agricultural pricing only when I was Chairman, APC. But anyway, the WTO doesn't go by Joshi or me using APC estimates. In fact, my critiques of the earlier Bank/WTO estimates were based on Tyagi's work. They go by the World Bank's estimates and the fact that some of our debates don't even understand this is sad. Fortunately, our negotiators at Doha did understand that neglect of protecting policy initiatives in the future which would emerge if the old taxing agriculture arguments were carried into the future would be dangerous for India. Now that we have negotiated a vantage position for ourself and full credit to Murasoli Maran and his team for that, the important issue is to prepare both for the negotiations in detail and for the actual trade, that would follow. As he has said, we gave up a little in the environment area, for advantages in agriculture. I would, in fact, put in more positively. To use an expression by Gary Simpson, who has written extensively on the WTO, we have introduced the concept of development in the WTO discussions on an operative level, we should, therefore, now be able to steer the environment and trade discussions to our advantage. This should most certainly be true for the agriculture sector and lends urgency to the arguments in this talk.

When in July the details of the discussion the US and the EU were coming out in driblets, it was clear that the pressure would be on us to reduce support to agriculture, when the negotiations begin seriously, which for us will be after Doha. Economists, bureaucrats and others, who said this would not happen, should look at the Chinese experience. China has the same arguments. They do not accept the estimates of subsidies the WTO uses, since their budgets use different concepts from those used, for example, by the IMF for government expenditure. The Chinese State Planning Commission has made this clear, as late as November, but China has accepted the negotiating position that subsidies to agriculture, currently estimated for WTO purposes at 10 per cent of agricultural GDP, will be brought down to 8.5 per cent, although the pressure was to reduce them to 5 per cent. In India's case, the clauses on food security, livelihood security and sustainable rural development will enable her to save that part of the policy system, which is worth saving. This is a big gain.

A number of our policies are not worth saving and that is our problem, but we have the space and the time in which we can reform ourself and that is important. In fact, if we are serious, next year's budget should be for the year of the WTO.

Subsidies to crops which are out of sync with demand both at home and abroad cannot be through procurement because you build up unwanted commodity mountains that way.

The real policy options then are to build markets, develop information systems of the economic opportunities available, provide financial institutions which work and provide finances for communication, processing, standardisation, quality upgradation and trade. Diversification is in any case not possible if the farmer does not have access to improved energy and water supplies and becomes much easier if the land development technologies are accessible. It is well known that he pays for such facilities when the service is good. Notice the queues when reliable energy is made available at a price. All of this means a great initiative to release the Indian farmer's energies by improving his access to inputs and services. It means market driven input supplies. This means that a number of organisations which cannot cover the last mile have to close down and this becomes difficult when they live on government subsidies and many others who succeed need to have access at least to bank finance. Cooperatives of the type we are pleading for have to be put in the driver's seat. The Rural Infrastructure Fund was meant to do this. But somewhere along the line it became a vehicle to finance the official irrigation plan. We have to revive it or develop a new vehicle to power the Indian farmer and his organisations to diversify, trade and improve his income. All of that will now be WTO compatible. After Doha, the main challenge is at home. The road map abroad is no longer hazy. Again, we have in the nineties agreed to very low tariff bounds for forest products, fruits, vegetables, dairy products from which the farm sector can make money. This is tragic and needs immediate reversal at the policy level.

The role of sponsoring policies for alternative distribution channels so that there is genuine competition in input supplies is not foreseen in Indian policy reform at all. Cooperatives, non-profit organisations and partnerships between private sector, Cooperatives, NGOs or local governments is not foreseen at all. A Committee that I chaired presented a draft law for cooperatives to set up producer companies with corporate alliances (See Alagh, 2000). It saved the cooperative principle by providing the one share one vote basis, but as V. Kurien and the Independent Cooperative Initiative declared in the Anand Declaration in December 2000, the legislation must be passed. It has now been tabled on the floor of Parliament by the Law Minister Arun Jaitley and we hope the Parliamentary Standing Committee under Pranab Mukherjee will support it.

There is a similar vast literature on irrigation performance and management systems. The struggle for defining rules which permit local initiative without open ended subsidies is being recognised. More important, there is now an awareness that there will now also have to be evolved a set of disincentives, in other words, rules which discourage perverse behaviour (See References, below for many case studies).

There is an interesting literature which is now emerging, which empirically questions the proposition that decentralisation and self management automatically increase performance levels. There can be a decline in government expenditures on the water sector. More important, there can be the lack of a policy focus which monitors performance and makes an effort to anticipate and develop systematic solutions to emerging problems. Empirical studies, therefore, show mixed results. The available results are of an extremely tentative nature needing systematic empirical study.

The literature on capacities and designs leads to interesting questions. On the one hand, it is argued that there has been an excessive emphasis on building physical capacities. Traditional management systems in particular, it is argued, are being swamped. On the other hand, it is argued that physical capacities have fallen short. The argument that the link between techno-managerial arrangements and local performance goals must be understood before measuring performance or proposing interventions probably contains an important clue. (Ambler, 1991, p.11). Alagh and Buch have shown that in planning distribution systems operating in the developed world needs a lot of innovative systems work. In the California Aqueduct or the Canal de Province, there were very few farmers as compared to the examples they studied. The behaviour of large farming populations then has to be studied and built into capacity and design parameters. Alagh and Buch (1995) show the use of acreage responses studies and water allocation and distribution systems working on conjunctive use principles with the operation authority monitoring and if necessary intervening. The Mekong Basin Indicative Plan asks for such work to be intensified. They refer to the Alagh-Buch modules, "an excellent example of how agricultural econometric models are used in water resource planning to help design and manage large irrigation systems" (Mekong River Commission, 1996). This is an area of high priority work for project design and policies.

While generally a recognition of water rights will lead to smaller dams, the need for basin and interbasin transfer of water will remain. For example, the stipulation in the Mekong agreement to cooperate on the maintenance of flows "to enable the acceptable natural reverse flow of the Tonle Sap to take place during the wet season". Agreement on the Cooperation for the Sustainable Development of the Mekong River Basin, (Art. 6) shows a sensitivity to water rights not seen earlier. These sensitivities will have important design and structural implications and work of an interdisciplinary nature not seen earlier, when the economist, the social anthropologist and the social worker were seen as add-ons after project design rather than a part of the engineering design team. Replication of these examples will need systematic work, training and manuals.

There are recent examples of difficult cultural issues being grossly mishandled by those who would know better. The important issue is that while socio-economic rehabilitation policies have been given priority, the underlying premises of the debates on sustainable development and rehabilitation have a strong developed country focus and very little effort is made to adjust institutions and the terms of debate to the structures of poor countries where the developments take place. This is a part of the larger failure to place reform debates in specific socio-cultural settings and therefore the lack of enduring change in institutions, including those in the water sector (Alagh, 1999).

On Limited Wants

A basic issue that has to be accepted in this century is that in spite of great technological progress of the kind that Gallopin and Colombo and others have outlined, the life style of the rich is simply not feasible for the world as a whole. Now that China and India are growing faster, this question which was raised at the Hague meeting by Gammini Correa cannot be avoided for long.

The notion that wants should be limited as a moral question is there in many religions. Yet most practical people find it unacceptable. In fact, the powerful counter factual is to the effect that given limited resources if everybody maximises his pleasure, the world will be the happiest possible place. In the early years of Independence, apart from morality these are the compulsion that saving rates were low and economic requirements were very pressing. It is now being argued that the concept of forced savings which is an outcome which is the other side of the coin of limited wants, is both unnecessary and inefficient, in the sense that it would misallocate resources. From this premise, it would follow that we should bravely go in for opening up India's consumer goods and service industries, for example, for international investment and competition.

The problem I suggest lies in another direction. Wants can be created today in such a manner that was never possible earlier. Modern communication is both an industry and a consumer product. It works with a devastating power and logic and profit seeking that goes behind itself. I am not against modern technology and modern communication. I think it is silly to keep on sticking to outdated technologies. In fact, I support the Department of Space when it says that it wants to leap frog and make its own facilities for the beaming of the latest messages on data products, communication and entertainment. I am proud of the fact that we have a Satellite Policy Document, which I have always whole-heartedly supported. Regulation, however, is important as our Satcom Policy shows for both cultural and economic reasons and is being followed across the globe since nations do tend to defend their cultural identities. The only prerequisite is that it must be transparent and fair.

The more serious questions on unrestricted pursuit of consumerism and utilitarian pleasure as universal objective arise from the fact that in a world of finite resources this is simply an unfeasible objective. Even if technical change continues at a pace at which it is continuing today it is extremely likely that by the time Chinese and Indian per capita levels cross around a quarter of the current levels in the United States, the world will destroy itself. As a Senior Advisor to the Secretary-General of the Rio Conference, I was given the privilege of being "one of 40 leading thinkers of the world", which prepared *The Hague Report on Sustainable Development : From Concept to Action*, as a part of the preparations that were done for the UN Conference on Environment and Development, by Mr. Maurice Strong. These "leaders" had to following say :

> "Sustainable development is concerned with models of material consumption which are replicable, while respecting cultural diversity. Such models recognise the limitations of environmental space. They do not treat ecospace as a tree good, to be plundered at the free will of any nation or any individual. They put a price on this space reflecting its relatively scarcity today and tomorrow. These models of development treat ecological space as any other scarce asset and are concerned with policies of sensible asset management."
>
> "At the global level, sustainable models of development require no less than a new global ethics, a clear understanding that the world cannot be made safe without the willing cooperation of everyone. Concern for common survival must also lead to policies for a more equitable order, based on fundamental global reform" and again
>
> "Out of such an unequal world on planet simply cannot emerge without some basic reforms. Nor can shared responsibility be created for the health of the Global Commons without some measure of shared global responsibility. Global sustainability without global justice will always remain an inclusive goal".

The UNCED Conference itself accepted this doctrine in the Rio Declaration in the following words :

> "Principle 8 : To achieve sustainable development and a higher quality of life for all people, States should reduce and eliminate unsustainable patterns of production and consumption and promote appropriate demographic policies".

I would suggest that India can afford to neglect this compulsion at considerable risk to its future. A more pressing concern is the fact the Planning Commission has brought out that not only public, but private savings are now falling and other things remaining the same this means a lower growth rate. The dream merchants seem to have sold the good life too soon.

Conclusion

The word coop, as a political scientist of the new emerging systems has argued, appears very often now. There are cooperative political arrangements at different levels of government, cooperation with non-governmental agencies, cooperative companies and cooperative arrangements with companies. Ismail Seragaldin has argued that developing countries will have to enter into contract arrangements for health and agriculture with the big genome companies in the private sector emerging at the beginning of this century. It seems to be recognised the world over that strategic alliances can be worked out as such that limited and focused degrees of community participation become the norm in the reform process. Decentralised market principles are easily grafted on this mode.

The falling profit rates in India agriculture need a fresh thinking. In a period when there has been large scale withdrawal of the state from input supplies, the rising input costs per unit require fresh design of institutions which supply the farm sector. In addition to corporate enterprises, these will be cooperative and community based organisations.

Removal of restrictions on trade will help agriculture and farmer based organisations. The net gains from trade may be small at the present stage, but are definitely worth internalising. Government policies towards newer strategic organisations like the Alagh Committee's proposals on corporate structures for cooperatives must be accepted rather than protecting the *sarkari* coops as the Independent Cooperative Initiative as argued.

The organisational and financial rules to make these arrangements and institutions effective will need considerable innovativeness. Problems of community collateral, recognition of hard budget constraints and yet flexibility at the local level, need policy coordination of a high order. Experience is that *mantras* of one or the other kind do not succeed. Hands on policy systems which monitor initial reform systems, anticipate and solve problems as they emerge and one can be sure that problems would emerge, are the preconditions of success as the ADBs Vision of Asian Agriculture estimates through a review of best practice cases (ADB, 2000). India needs to develop such a perspective.

(This is revised version of a Foundation Day Lecture at NIRD).

References

Alagh, Y. (1979): Task Force on Minimum Need and Effective Demand, See Government of India, 1979, below.

——— *et al.*, (1984): Policy Modelling for Planning in India, in E. Thorbeeke, ed., below.

——— (1988): Guidelines for Agroclimatic Planning: A Draft for Discussion, *Journal of Land Development*.

——— (1991): Indian Development Planning and Policy, *WIDER Studies in Development Economics*, Helsinki and Delhi, Vikas.

——— (1991): Sustainable Development, From Concept to Action: *Techniques for Planners*, UNCED.

——— and M. Khattab (1993): *Food Security Information System for Arab Republic of Egypt*, Vol. 3, (Models), Cairo, FAO.

——— (1994): Planning and Policies for Indian Agricultural Research, 25th Lal Bahadur Shastri Lecture, reprinted in ICAR, *Landmarks in Indian Agriculture*.

——— *Next Phase of Agricultural Research*, in ARPU volume 2 of same title, New Delhi, Concept.

Alagh, Y. and D. Buch (1995): The SSP and Sustainable Development, in W. Fisher, Columbia University Seminars, below.

——— (2000): Water and Food Security in South Asia, invited *Plenary Lecture at World Water Forum and Ministerial Meeting*, Hague.

——— (2000): Report of the High Level Committee on Legislation for Corporatisation of Cooperatives, New Delhi, Ministry of Company Affairs.

——— (2000): *Sustainable Development* : India 2020, Tokyo, UNU/IAS

——— (2000): *Popular Participation and Planning* : Case Studies, Bangkok, U.N. ESCAP Transport Bulletin.

——— (2001): Working out Power Economics, *Indian Express*, Jan. 16.

Ambler, J. (1991): Bounding the System, in IMMI, below, pp. 3-12.

Alexandratos, N. (Ed), (1995): *World Agriculture Towards 2010*, An FAO Study, Chichister, Wiley.

Asian Development Bank (ADB), (1999): *The Growth and Sustainability of Agriculture in Asia*, Manila, ADB.

ADB (2000): *Rural Asia : Bey and the Green Revolution*, Manila ADB.

ADB (2000): *Rural Asia : Companion Volumes* (I-III), Oxford University Press, UNU/IAS.

Chopra, K. and G. Kadekodi, (1993): Watershed Development, *Economic and Political Weekly*, June 26, pp. A61-A67.

Chambers, R. (1998): *Managing Canal Irrigation : Practical Analysis from South Asia*, Cambridge University Press.

De Los Reves and S. Jopillo (1987): An Evaluation of NIA's Participatory Communal Programme, in IMMI, below.

FAO (1978/81, 1982): *Agro-Economic Zoning Atlas*, Rome, FAO-UNESCO.

FAO (1993): *Agriculture Towards 2010*, Rome, FAO, for final published version, see N. Alexandratos.

Fisher, W. (1995): *Towards Sustainable Development*, Columbia University Seminar Series, New York, Sharpe.

Gangrade, K.D. and N. Radhakrishnan, (Ed) (2000): *Gandhi and The Changing Facets of India*, See paper by Y.K. Alagh, Gandhi and the Indian Economy the 21st Century, pp. 44-62, New Delhi, Gandhi Smriti.

Government of India, (1979): Planning Commission, P.P.D., *Report of the Task Force on Projections of Minimum Needs and Effective Consumption*, New Delhi, P.P.D.

——— (1989): *Agro Climatic Planning : An Overview*, New Delhi. Planning Commission authorship, Y.K. Alagh (*et.al*)

——— (2000): Commission on Agricultural Costs and Prices, *Reports for the Crops Sown for the 1999/2000 Session*

Helleiner, G. (1986): *Balance of Payments Experience and Growth Prospects in Developing Countries*, World Development, Vol. 14, pp. 877-908.

Hayaami, Y. (1981): Understanding Village Community and the Direction of Agricultural Change in Asia, Delhi, IEG, Occasional Paper, New Series No. 1

International Institute of Irrigation Management (IIIM) (1987): *Public Interventions in Farmer Managed Irrigation Systems*, Colombo IIIM

——— (1991): *Performance Measurement in Farmer Managed Irrigation Systems, Colombo*, IIIM

Joshi, Sharad (2000): What Price Alagh Economics, *Business Line*, December 20

Korten, D. (Ed) (1986): *Community Management : Asian Experience and Perspective*, New Haven, Kumarian

Lele, U., N. Kumar, Y. Alagh, N. Saxena and K. Mitra (2000): *Forestry in India : An Evaluation*, Washington, World Bank

Lindert, P. (1996): *The Bad Earth*, Davis, UCAL Agricultural History Centre

Manor, S, and J. Chambouleyron 1991, in IIIM above

Mitra, Saumya Kanti (2001): *Ajanta and China, Economics Times*, Jan. 19

Nasution, I. (1993): *Agricultural Regionalisation of Indonesia*, Bogor, Agricultural Research Centre

NABARD, (1991): Annual Report, Bombay NABARD, See on financing agroclimatic development

Ostrom, I. (1994): *Neither Market Nor State : Governance of Common Pool Resources*, Washington, IFPRI

——— *et al.* (1996): Rules, *Games and Common Pool Resources*, Ann Arbor, University of Michighan Press

Pronk, J. and M. Haq (1992): *Sustainable Development : From Concept to Action*, UNCED and UNDP

Sachs, I. (1991): Background Paper for the Hague Declaration, extensively reprinted in Nature and by RIS

Sadasyuk, G., and P. Sengupta (1968): *Economic Regionalisation of India : Problems and Approaches*, New Delhi, Census of India, Monograph No. 8 of Census 1960

Siy, R., Averting Bureaucratisation of a Community Managed Resource, in D.C. Korten, above

Small, L., and I. Carruthers (1991): *Farmer Financed Irrigation*, Cambridge University Press

Sonntag, N. (1996): Adaptive Management Policy Exercises : Two Methods for Integrated Resource Management, in MRC above, p. 27

United Nations, UNU/IAS, Papers read at *Conference on Sustainable Future of the Global System*, Tokyo

Vaidya, C. (1999): Private Sector Participation in Financing and Management of Urban Water Supply and Sanitation Projects, Delhi USUAID FIRI : Project, reprinted in 31st *Annual IWWA Technical Volume*

Vermillon, D. (1997): *Impacts of Irrigation Management Transfer : A Review of the Evidence*, Colombo, IIIM

Wade, R. (1982): *Employment, Water Control and Water Supply Institutions*, Sussex, IDS.

5

Let the Sun Shine on the Grassroots Too: 73rd Constitutional Amendment

Story of Implementation and Deviations

Nirmala Buch

INTRODUCTION

In India, village Panchayats have been traditional institutions of local governance and community level dispute resolution based on social consensus. Their decline and superimposition of costly formal courts led to realization of their important role and, therefore, efforts were started for their formal, statutory revival in colonial period itself. In independent India, the directive principles of state policy in Article 40 of the Constitution exhorted the states to take steps to organize village Panchayats and endow them with such powers and authority as may be necessary to enable them to function as units of self-government. The three decades of nineteen fifties to nineteen eighties saw phases of revival and neglect of these vital grass-roots institutions of local governance with heavy social and political costs for the rural areas. The patchy progress of development initiatives, lack of people's participation and support led to realization of the need to deepen democracy and develop inclusive and capable institutions of local governance.

The 73rd Constitutional Amendment in 1992 adding Part IX to the Constitution for mandating vibrant Panchayat institutions drew upon the efforts made by different states to organize Panchayats in the four decades since the Constitution became effective. It sought to include essential features for their continuous existence with more inclusive membership and with adequate powers and resources. It also included a complete three-tier Panchayati Raj structure instead of village Panchayats only as initially expected in Article 40 as an essential uniform structure for the whole country. Even with these features included in the Constitution itself by this Amendment the subject of Panchayats still continues to be within the competence of the states. Hence, a number of steps to implement these provisions had to be finally fashioned by the state legislatures while bringing their Panchayat legislations in conformity with this Amendment.

The Amendment of 1992 was not applicable to certain states/areas with tribal population which required special features for their local administration. Article 243 M stipulated that this amendment was not applicable to Scheduled Areas specified in Schedule V and tribal areas specified in Schedule VI to the Constitution. While in the states of Nagaland, Meghalaya and Mizoram, their state legislatures were given powers to apply this Amendment to their non-Schedule VI Areas, the powers to apply it to Schedule V Areas were left to the Parliament which it could do by special legislation including any required exceptions and modifications. Parliament passed this legislation in 1996. Hence, the states had to later amend their Panchayat laws to conform to this legislation — "The provisions of the Panchayats (Extension to the Scheduled Areas) Act, 1996" by which the provisions of Part IX were extended to Schedule V Areas with certain modifications relating to the protection of tribal customs and practices, more access and control to the local tribal community over natural resources and on certain social institutions besides much larger guaranteed positions for tribals in the leadership of Panchayats.

We intend to analyse in this chapter, how various states have conformed to the letter and spirit of the 73rd Constitutional Amendment and of the 1996 Act extending the provisions of panchayats to the Schedule V Areas. We intend to especially see the deviations with reference to the core issues and features of these two enactments.

THE CORE FEATURES OF THE AMENDMENT

The essential core features of the Amendment are related to the mandated composition, election, life, powers, resources and the autonomy of Panchayats as institutions of self-government. These can be summarized as follows to enable us to test the actions taken in the states:

(1) *Composition and regular elections*

(a) Three-tier Panchayat structure throughout the rural areas of all the states except those to which Article 243-M gives exemption but with future expectation of action by Parliament and/or legislatures of those states for its application. A two-tier structure in smaller states with population up to two lakhs.
(b) Fixed five years' tenure for all Panchayats and their office bearers with no powers to extend this period as was being done earlier by the state governments extending the period for one reason or the other and thereby avoiding/delaying regular elections.
(c) Elections to all Panchayats by independent State Election Commissions to be set up by the states.
(d) All Panchayat memberships to be by direct election from territorial constituencies of the Panchayat area i.e. no nominations or cooptions etc. The only exception given for ex-officio membership of MPs/MLAs and to presidents of lower tier Panchayats in the higher level Panchayat bodies.
(e) For chairpersons, the state Panchayat legislations can provide for election of chairpersons of the village Panchayats directly by all voters or indirectly by the members of the Panchayats but chairpersons of the district level and intermediate level Panchayats are to be elected by their members only.
(f) Reservations for weaker sections of SC/ST and for women in the membership as well as in the

chairpersons' posts – for SC/ST proportionate to their population and for women not less than one-third of the members/chairpersons posts. Women's minimum one-third reservation to be not only in total seats of a Panchayat or total number of chairpersons at a level but also among those reserved for SC/ST separately. With the 1996 law, all chairpersons to Panchayats in Schedule V Areas have to be tribals and their members to have fifty per cent tribal members.

(2) *Devolution of powers and functions* to enable Panchayats to function as institutions of self-government (more than only units of self-government expected in Article 40 earlier) and to prepare plans and implement schemes for economic development and social justice including but not limiting to the items listed in Schedule XI added with this Amendment. The 1996 law mandates extensive powers over the natural resources, social sector institutions, etc.

(3) *A mandatory Gram Sabha*, a body of all voters of the village with functions as may be prescribed, with village defined as the area for which a village Panchayat is to be constituted.

(4) *Recognition of Panchayats as self-governing institutions* with domain without interference, control and encroachment.

(5) *Financial Resources* to Panchayats for the functions and responsibilities entrusted to them and including the institutional mechanisms of State Finance Commission to be set up in every state every five years and the role of the Central Finance Commission for recommending resources transfer to Panchayati Raj Institutions.

(6) *District Planning Committee* in each district for the purpose of collating the plans prepared by the Panchayats and municipalities and giving them to the state government for action.

Inherent in these essential provisions is a vision of vibrant, active Panchayats with more inclusive membership across caste, class and gender, responsive and responsible to the local community, with resources and with powers to raise resources to fulfil their responsibilities and to meet the needs and aspirations of the local population. Hence, we can see the desirability of moving beyond the minimum reservations and devolution of functions delineated in this Amendment. Thus the one-third reservation for women is only "not less than" and may be increased to more without any maximum or in proportion to their share in the population. The devolution of powers and functions too is not limited to the XI Schedule, which has an indicative list of 29 items and subjects for transfer to PRIs. The financial resources given to the Panchayats need not be limited to the devolution recommended by a State Finance Commission. Further, though the State Finance Commission recommendations are not automatically fully binding, there is expectation of evolution of a convention to expeditiously accept and implement them as has already developed for the Central Finance Commission for sharing and distribution of resources between the centre and the states. Functioning of the Panchayat bodies is expected to be not as mere agencies implementing state structured programmes/ schemes, whether centrally sponsored or state schemes, but to be responsive, responsible local government institutions.

There are also certain permissible features which have been left to the discretion of the state legislatures. Thus, they can give reservation to other Backward Classes. As exceptions to the general prescription for only elected members in Panchayats, the state Panchayat laws can include MPs, MLAs and MLCs as ex-officio members of the Panchayats at the district and intermediate levels. The chairpersons of the Panchayats at the village and intermediate levels can be made ex-officio members of the next higher level Panchayat body to provide an organic link among them for their functions.

The 1996 law, extending the Panchayat provisions to Schedule V Areas adds certain essential features for Panchayats in areas of tribal concentration in the states of PP, Bihar (undivided), Gujarat, HP, MP (undivided), Maharashtra, Orissa and Rajasthan. These include leadership positions of all Panchayats at all levels to be with tribals only, fifty per cent of their members to be tribals, overarching role of the Gram Sabha, preservation of tribal customs and traditions, control over natural resources, minor forest produce and minor minerals which are crucial for tribal livelihood, control over social sector institutions and functionaries in the area to manage them in the interest of tribals' special needs. This law is focusing more on the Gram Sabha and also provides for a Gram Sabha in every village or habitation instead of a Gram Sabha for the whole village Panchayat area. However, it also leaves a number of matters relating to allocation of specific powers to appropriate level Panchayats to the state legislatures.

THE EXPECTATIONS AND GROUND REALITIES

The philosophy of "power" to the people at the grassroots was the guiding principle of these two Constitutional enactments. Their main objective was to strengthen the PRIs throughout the country and make them "institutions of self government" with responsibility of promoting economic development and ensuring social justice. Therefore, the Amendment provided for devolution of powers, functions and finances, access to weaker sections in society to power at the grassroots level and making the PRIs financially strong so that they can perform meaningful role in overall development. The experience of implementation of various provisions and the situation that has emerged over the last seven years of working of the PRIs in the revised set-up in different states raises certain questions regarding the expectations and ground realities. The extent of success in achieving devolution of powers, functions and finances, in empowerment of weaker sections in the society in general and women's empowerment in particular need to be seen, besides the functioning of newly established organs like the State Election Commissions and the State Finance Commissions and the overall attitude of the political leadership and bureaucracy towards these changes.

The provisions in the 73rd Constitutional Amendment Act, 1992 include mandatory items and some discretionary items. Although most of the mandatory items contained in the 73rd Amendment have been accepted and implemented in letter by the state governments, there are "deviations" or infirmities while implementing various provisions mandatory as well as discretionary, which go against the spirit of democratic decentralization inherent in this Amendment. We look at these infirmities in the context of the core features of the Amendment and the 1996 law extending these provisions to the Schedule V Areas. We see them with reference to (a) Panchayats' organization, representation and reservation, (b) devolution of powers and functions, (c) district planning committees, and (d) the increasing trend of creation of parallel, alternate structures for delivery of development programmes and people's participation instead of using the Panchayat structure.

Organisation, Representation and Reservation

All the states have legislated to provide for organisation of Panchayats at three (or two in states with up to 20 lakh population) levels and for direct elections to their membership with reservations as mandated in the Amendment. However, there are deviations and additions which are against the letter as well as the spirit of the Amendment. No membership is possible now by co-option or nomination except the ex-officio membership of MLAs/MPs/MLCs in district and intermediate level Panchayats and of chairpersons of lower level Panchayats in the next higher level Panchayat bodies. But in Andhra Pradesh, Section 149 of the state law includes co-option of one person from the minority community in the Mandal Panchayat and Section 171 includes co-option of two members of the minority community in the Zila Parishad. The legal validity of these co-options does not seem to have been questioned in any courts so far but these clearly violate Article 243C (2) that all Panchayat members will be directly elected from territorial constituencies. The Punjab State Panchayat Act of 1994 as originally enacted stipulated that 40 per cent of the members of the Panchayat Samities were to be elected directly by the voters and 60 per cent indirectly by and from amongst the Sarpanchs of the Samiti area. It has been changed recently, but only to make it 50 per cent direct and 50 per cent indirect election. This is again a clear violation in letter as well as in spirit of the provisions of Article 243C introduced by the 73rd Constitutional Amendment. Further, Gram Sabha areas have been constituted for village Panchayats, but wards in the Gram Sabha area have not been demarcated. So, in case of re-election of Panchs to vacant seats irrespective of the reason, the total voters of Gram Sabha area will have to vote again for a Panch seat. This is against the clear provision of Article 243C (2) that the members have to be elected from individual territorial constituencies.

Another deviation is in West Bengal Panchayat Act in respect of ex-officio membership of members of Panchayat Samities and Zila Parishads in Gram Panchayats and Panchayat Samities, respectively, located within their individual constituencies. One view on the subject is that even though the constitutional validity of this provision is doubtful, it is a harmless one, and it contributes towards strengthening integration of different tiers. Andhra Pradesh also has made a provision that members of the Mandal Parishad territorial constituency of the area will be permanent invitees in the Gram Panchayat with right to speak though having no right to vote [Section 7 (2) in the Andhra Pradesh Act 1994].

In Madhya Pradesh, the Panchayat, law as initially enacted in 1993 provided for co-options of representatives of SCs/STs and cooperative societies in the Gram Panchayats, ex-officio membership of chairpersons of district cooperative bodies and district cooperative banks and co-option of director of cooperative marketing society or of a cooperative bank and of members of SCs/STs in Janpad Panchayats and Zila Panchayats. These, of course, were removed by an amending ordinance during the first Panchayat elections in 1994 and hence, rectified. Another feature added by the MP Panchayat Act is to permit the MPs and MLAs to send their representatives if they cannot attend the meetings of district or block level panchayats of which they are ex-officio members. Though the rules stipulate that such a representative will be attending when the MP/MLA concerned is unable to attend, in practice they become their standing representatives. Numerous references to the assertiveness and powers of such representatives and various hoardings speaking of foundation stones laid/ inaugurations of works by them as MPs' representatives indicate their alternative centres of power. These cannot be seen as following the spirit of the 73rd Amendment.

While the reservation in case of members as well as of chairpersons of any PRI is for their full term i.e. five years in all the states, it has been changed to a shorter duration in the case of chairperson's office in some states. For example, in Maharashtra in the case of chairpersons of Zila Parishad, though the term of office is five years, the chairmanship was effectively changed to one year as it was rotated every year among all reserved categories. As it was a very short tenure, it has been changed later to two and half years. In Karnataka, it has been changed to 20 months, so the chairmanship is rotated after this period and one tenure of five years will see three chairpersons. The Amendment stipulated mandatory rotation of reservations of chairpersons' posts in a manner prescribed. It is this reference to "prescribed manner" that these states have used to ensure that there is no evolution of new leadership from the new entrants from the social groups who have entered these posts in significant number through reservations for the first time at this level.

The 73rd Amendment provides for reservation of SCs/STs in proportion to their as far as the membership is concerned and in the total for chairmanship. Article 243D (1) reads as follows: "The number of seats so reserved shall bear, as nearly as may be, the same proportion to the total number of seats to be filled by direct election in that Panchayat as the population of the Scheduled Castes in that Panchayat area or of the Scheduled Tribes in that Panchayat area bears to the total population of that area ......" 243D (4) about chairpersons says: "The number of offices of chairpersons reserved for the Scheduled Castes and the Scheduled Tribes in the Panchayats at each level in any state shall bear, as nearly as may be, the same proportion to the total number of such offices in the Panchayats at each level as the population of the Scheduled Castes in the State or of the Scheduled Tribes in the State bears to the total population of the State".

In the Madhya Pradesh Panchayat Law, posts of Sarpanchs of Gram Panchayats are to be reserved for SC/ST in proportion to their population and posts of Presidents of Janpad Panchayats in proportion to their population in the district. Only in the Zila Panchayats, these are to be reserved in proportion to their population in the state [Section 17 (2) for Gram Panchayat, 25 (2) for Janpad Panchayat and 32 (2) for Zila Panchayats]. This has resulted in giving reservations to SC/ST in the posts of presidents of Janpad and Zila Panchayats differently than what would be permissible when based on the proportionate population in the state. Thus, while the population of SC and ST in the state is 14.55 per cent and 23.99 per cent respectively (1911 Census), the reservation of Janpad Panchayat president posts for SC/ST in the state were 13.94 per cent and 32.03 per cent and for Gram Panchayat Sarpanch 14.56 per cent and 29.20 per cent for 1994 elections. In the 2000 elections, the reservations for SC in Janpad Panchayat presidents were 11.55 per cent and Gram Panchayat Sarpanch 12.95 per cent. We are not calculating for ST for this election as by this time the 1996 law extending Panchayats provisions to Schedule V Areas gave them 100 per cent of these posts in the Schedule V Areas in the state. It may be noted that unlike in the case of women where one-third is only at least for SC/ST, it has to be as far as may be proportionate to their population in the state and not more or less by using a formula or basis different from what is specifically provided in the Constitutional Amendment itself, namely, proportionate population in the area and state for members and chairpersons, respectively. So the state law should have provided for reserving that number at the state level and then distributing them to the districts, blocks according to their population of these social groups and not aggregating them after providing differently at the local level. Such a procedure also distributes the reservation in areas/

districts differently than their share in accordance with the clear Constitutional mandate.

Some of the states have also given additional reservations, which is in line with the intent of the amendment. Thus, M.P. law provides that if the president of a Zila Panchayat or Janpad Panchayat or Sarpanch of a Gram Panchayat is not SC/ST or OBC, then the vice president of Zila Panchayat [Section 32 (4)], the vice president of Janpad Panchayat [Section 25 (4)] and Up-sarpanch of gram panchayat [Section 17 (6)] has to be from SC/ST/OBC categories. In West Bengal and Orissa, reservations have been given to women among vice presidents of the Panchayats. These are positive additions in accordance with the spirit and expectations of the 73rd Amendment. However, combining the SC/ST/OBC in the case of MP state is a combination of unequals and is skewed in favour of OBC as against SC/ST who are more disadvantaged politically, socially and economically.

Another deviation from the 73rd Amendment in respect of representation is in Himachal Pradesh where the law provided for direct election of the Up-sarpanch of Gram Panchayat from the whole Panchayat area. As he is neither a simple member who could be from a territorial constituency nor a chairperson who can be from the whole Panchayat area, this is a questionable provision. Himachal Pradesh provides another deviation in the quorum of the Gram Sabha. The spirit and philosophy of the Panchayat law and practice as well as for other democratic institutions is for representation of individual voters in various fora. But by a recent amendment in the Himachal Pradesh Act in 2000, the quorum in the Gram Sabha can be representation of "one-third of the total number of families represented by one or more members of the Gram Sabha area" and for the adjourned meeting it will be "one-fifth of the total number of families represented by one or more members of the Gram Sabha". The family is defined here as a "a joint family of all persons descended from common ancestor including adoption, who live, worship and mess together permanently as shown in the Gram Panchayat". This definition of the family is a questionable concept as it may exclude some voters and particularly women whose other responsibilities and constraints affect their ability to come for various meetings.

In terms of representation, another deviation is seen in the various disqualifications provided for election to the Panchayats, as these would debar a large number of persons who would be entering Panchayats for the first time after the reservations given there. These deviations against the spirit of the 73rd Amendment include the eligibility criterion of "two child norm" that any one having more than two children after a specified date cannot contest or continue as a representative in the Panchayat at any level. Andhra Pradesh, Haryana, Rajasthan and Orissa included this disqualification in their laws enacted in 1993. The states of Madhya Pradesh (undivided) and Himachal Pradesh have introduced it in 2000. Recent studies of this experience have shown how this law adversely affects the new young entrants to Panchayats, especially women and weaker sections whom the 73rd Amendment has sought to bring in Panchayats through the reservations across caste, class and gender (MCM: 2003).

Irregular elections despite the clear tenure of five years from the first meeting of a Panchayat stipulated in the Amendment has been attempted in a number of states and the matter had to go to the High Courts and Supreme Court before the second set of Panchayat elections were organized in these states. Thus, Karnataka and Andhra Pradesh delayed their elections with AP raising the issue of the three/two upper levels of Panchayats and the direct/indirect elections of their members. Karnataka suddenly felt the need to review the delimitation of constituencies rather late when the elections were to be organized again. In Madhya Pradesh, the whole matter of reservation was taken, of course, by an individual petitioner to the High Court, questioning the high percentage of reservations, especially for tribals in the tribal areas. The High Court stayed the elections but vacated the stay after six months. So the elections were held in January-February 2000, instead of June 1999. The local perception was that the whole process to delay the elections by using the legal proceeding was because it did not suit the political parties in the state to have the elections before the Parliament elections suddenly called in 1999.

In Orissa, when the ruling party changed in the elections to the state legislature, the Panchayats were dissolved through a resolution in the state legislature, using the powers in Article 243 N introduced by the 73rd Amendment but then the elections were postponed again and again on various grounds including the ground of drought conditions in the state. The elections were then held only after continuous civil society pressure and the court case. In Punjab, a tenure of five years for all the three tiers of the Panchayati Raj system has been enacted in the Punjab Panchayat Act in accordance with the Constitutional Amendment. So, the elections to Panchayat Samities and Zila Parishads were due in October 1999. But these have not been held till date, thus violating the timeframe of five years duration.

Another deviation in practice, though not stipulated in any enactment, relates to the elections to the chairpersons of district and intermediate levels. In some of the states, these elections are not conducted by the State Election Commissions. These are conducted by the government machinery. Madhya Pradesh, Maharashtra and Karnataka come in this category, while in the states of Orissa and UP, these elections are organised by the State Election Commissions. The argument in the former group of states is that the direct elections will be organised by the State Election Commission but as these elections of chairpersons are indirect elections by the members of these bodies, these will be organised by the state governments. If this argument is accepted, then the Rajya Sabha elections will not be organized by the Election Commission of India. This position, therefore, needs to be corrected and all states must have elections to Panchayats, of their members as well as chairpersons, whether direct or indirect, organised only by the State Election Commissions.

The constitutional amendment speaks of the delimitation of constituencies and also makes it clear that validity of a law relating to this subject cannot be questioned by any court of law (Article 243 O). Delimitation of constituencies has, therefore, been done by the executive governments from time to time and has not always been seen as fair and objective. The case of Uttar Pradesh had to go to the High Court and Supreme Court before the first Panchayat elections could take place in 1995. It would be desirable if the delimitation of the constituencies is entrusted to a Delimitation Commission or given to the State Election Commissions instead of leaving it to the executive authority of the concerned states where politics of the political leaders at higher levels influences various decisions.

Devolution of Powers and Functions

Article 243 G expects the state legislatures to examine various subjects in detail and entrusts powers and responsibilities to the Panchayats in respect of as many subjects as may be appropriate, keeping in view the spirit of the Amendment and local conditions. The states may also take a view as suggested in various fora on merging the DRDAs with the District Panchayats if deemed fit. The Report of the first Maharashtra State Finance Commission (1997) had recommended that "poverty" alleviation subjects may be transferred to the Panchayat bodies, but the state government rejected this recommendation on the ground that if this recommendation was accepted, the entire structure of DRDA would have to be abolished. But this cannot be an adequate justification to reject this recommendation. The staffing as appropriate can be made available to the ZPs. In fact, the problem lies in the reluctance to transfer of control and authority from state government to the Panchayat bodies, i.e. Zila Parishads at the district level. In any case, Karnataka abolished DRDAs long ago and MP has also merged them in the Zila Panchayats without any problem. But even the Ministry of Rural Development, Government of India, continues to change its views on such merger from time to time.

The first Punjab Finance Commission in 1995 recommended some functional and financial powers in favour of PRIs and local bodies, for social justice and economic development. The state government did not implement the recommendations and constituted the Second Finance Commission for further recommendations and the 29 subjects mentioned in the IX Schedule of the Act on the lines of the XI Schedule to the Constitution have not been transferred to the PRIs in Punjab.

The State Legislature in Maharashtra has not devolved all the powers and authority to enable the Panchayats to function as institutions of self government. According to the report of the First Maharashtra State Finance Commission (1997), nine subjects included in the Eleventh Schedule of the Constitution had not been transferred to Panchayat bodies: (i) Land development and land consolidations, (ii) Fisheries, (iii) Minor forest produce, (iv) Small scale industries (including food processing), khadi and cottage industries, (v) Rural electrification (including distribution), (vi) Technical and professional education, (vii) Adult education and non-formal education, (viii) Public distribution system (PDS) and (ix) Land improvement of these, the subject of adult education and non-formal education has been transferred to PRIs very recently. From recent press reports it appears that some of the ministers as well as staff working in these departments have opposed the transfer of these subjects to the Panchayat bodies on various grounds.

In many states, specific subjects are entrusted to the Panchayats by listing them in the legislation relating to Panchayati Raj. But in Tamil Nadu, this has been made merely by a notification. No powers have been given to Panchayats in Tamil Nadu for the management and control of delivery of social services and basic needs and development functions like education, health, PDS, agriculture, land, etc. The state government claims that powers need to be devolved step by step. In reality, if we examine the government orders related to the 29 items we see that only limited power has been delegated like "to report to the appropriate authority", "identification of beneficiaries", "assisting the departments", etc.

States have not been very generous about devolution of powers and functions to the Panchayats or in giving them adequate resources. The entrustment of functions has also been changed from time to time. Thus, for instance, in Madhya

Pradesh, Section 53 of the Panchayat Act provides that the state government may, by general or special order, entrust to the Panchayats preparation of plans and implementation of schemes of economic development and social justice including those in relation to the matters listed in Schedule V which is a reproduction of Schedule XI added by the 73rd Amendment. However, sub-section (2) to this section also provided that the state government may by general or special order add to any of the functions of the Panchayats or withdraw the functions and duties entrusted to such Panchayats, when the state government undertakes the execution of any of the functions entrusted to panchayats. While it is understandable that the Panchayats are not sovereign bodies and have to work within the overall policy of the state government, their autonomy and action within their jurisdiction need to be ensured so that they can work with responsibility, confidence and authority. Their functions and resources should not be changed from time to time. Hence, this sub-section is against the spirit of the Amendment.

FINANCIAL RESOURCES OF PRIS

Article 243 H mentions powers to impose taxes by and raising/ receiving of funds of the Panchayats. The mandatory part of this Article refers to the constitution of State Finance Commissions within one year. The report of the Commission has to be laid before the legislature of the state along with reports of action taken on these recommendations. The states set up their Finance Commissions on various dates though some with delays. The Commissions took a long time in completing their reports and some of the state governments took even longer to take decisions thereon.

The Governor of Maharashtra, for instance, constituted the first Maharashtra State Finance Commission on 23rd April, 1994. The State Finance Commission submitted its report to the state government on 31st January, 1997, that means almost after a period of 2 years and 9 months of its constitution. The state government placed this report on the table of the state legislature along with its Action Taken Report (ATR) on 5th March, 1999, that means the state government further took almost over 2 years and 2 months for consideration of this report. This inordinate delay at various levels is indicative of deviation from the spirit of Article 243 H of the Constitution.

The state government in its action taken report mentioned that out of a total number of 129 recommendations made by the State Finance Commission, four had been totally rejected, eleven had been partially accepted, and others had been fully accepted. One of the four rejected recommendations related to sharing of the Professional Tax between the state government on the one hand and the Gram Panchayats/Municipalities on the other. This recommendation was made to strengthen the financial position of the Gram Panchayats in the state. Unfortunately, as this recommendation has been rejected, the financial position of Gram Panchayats is likely to remain weak, even in future.

The first State Finance Commission of West Bengal in its report submitted in 1995 recommended that 16 per cent of the net revenue of the state government should be transferred to the Panchayats in an untied form. The Commission further suggested that the various line departments should transfer to the Panchayats such of their schemes which are of local nature and do not have implications for more than one district. The Panchayats could have acquired sufficient autonomy had these recommendations been implemented. But, till recently, the government sat over these recommendations. In 1999-2000 and in 2000-01, the state government took some steps to implement them. But the implementation falls much short of the recommendations, as evidenced in the release of only a token amount as untied fund in the last financial year and no release in the previous year.

District Planning Committees: Constitution and Structure

In the 74th Amendment, Article 243 Z D was added to provide for District Planning Committees (DPCs) to collate the plans prepared by Panchayats and municipalities in the district to prepare draft plan for the district and to send it to the state government. This provision has had lukewarm compliance in most of the states. A number of states have not constituted DPCs so far. Thus the District Planning Committees have not been constituted in Punjab and, therefore, only District Planning Boards are working in all the districts. The District Planning Committees (DPCs) have not been constituted in AP too. The Chief Planning Officer is still the nodal officer for planning in the district. Meanwhile, the "Janmabhoomi" programme has been launched in the state with great expectations. It is aimed at participatory planning process at the micro levels (Shastry: 1999).

Some of the other states, who have constituted the DPCs, have changed their compositions and scope of work beyond the intention of the Constitutional Amendment. Thus, while Kerala has made it the instrument of a people's plan, Madhya Pradesh has made it an agency subordinate to the state government by a law for the purpose of powers given to it for various government functions. Madhya Pradesh has called it "district government" and made the minister in charge of the district as chairperson of the DPC. Hence, in practice, it has become an institution, which undermines the whole intention of making the three-tier Panchayat structure headed by the Zila Panchayat as the institutional structure of self-government. The chairperson of the Zila Panchayat is only one member of this committee and with collector as secretary of DPC and the CEO of the Zila Parishad as Additional Collector of the district, it beautifully undermines the authority of the Zila Panchayat. Some other states too e.g. Himachal Pradesh and Maharashtra have followed the example by making a minister from the state government as chairperson of this committee. Tamil Nadu is in a class by itself where the collector was made the chairperson of the DPC. There was widespread criticism of this decision. Finally, the Finance Minister's (Chief Minister's) budget speech on 24th March, 2000 mentioned that the District Planning Committees will hereafter function under the chairmanship of the District Panchayat chairpersons instead of District Collectors.

In Maharashtra, the state government has abolished the earlier District Planning and Development Councils (DPDCs) and in their place, constituted the District Planning Committees (DPCs), but the economic plans are still prepared by the officers of the concerned departments of the state government. It was envisaged in Article 243 ZD that the plans be prepared first at the grassroots level, and then at the intermediate and district levels, with the participation of people at these levels. This process of planning as well as implementation has not been effected in Maharashtra so far. In the new set-up, it was expected that the chairperson of the Zila Parishad should be the chairperson of the District Planning Committee (DPC), but here too like MP and HP the guardian minister of the district continues to chair the DPC.

Parallel, Alternative Structures and Responsibilities

The MPs Local Area Development Scheme (MPLADS) announced by the then Prime Minister in both Houses of Parliament on 23 December, 1993 is the most significant development against the spirit of the 73rd Amendment. Each Member of Parliament has the freedom to suggest to the District Collector, works to be done with a sum not exceeding Rs. 1 crore per year within his or her constituency. Twenty-three specific schemes such as construction of school buildings, village roads, bridges, common shelters for the old, buildings for Gram Panchayats, hospitals or cultural/sport activities, digging of tube wells, etc., besides any other scheme specified by the Union Government from time to time, fall under the Local Area Development Scheme. The Central Government releases the funds to the District Collector who operates it. Rupees ten lakh is the maximum for any single work. Subsequently, the total amount was increased to Rs. 2 crores. There have also been recent moves to increase the amount to Rs. 3 crores for each MP. The scheme is available to Members of Rajya Sabha too who can use it in any constituency in their state. The Scheme violates the spirit of the 73rd Constitutional Amendment. The XI Schedule (Article 243 G) and XII Schedule (Article 243 W) contain the list of 47 subjects that should devolve to the local governments. Interestingly, all the 23 items of work meant to be implemented with the guidance of MPs under MPLADS are from the 29 subjects of the XI Schedule. Several reports have suggested that the MPLADS funds were misused or remained unutilized.

A similar scheme has been launched in some states for the MLAs and MLCs as well. This is also an inroad in the domain of local bodies. Thus, the MLAs in Maharashtra are given Rs. 60 lakh every year to undertake development works in their constituencies. These are discretionary funds and are utilised by the persons concerned according to their choice and convenience. In MP, the MLAs are given Rs. 25 lakhs every year. This goes against the basic principle of accountability and may lead to imbalance in development in the district. To make the decentralisation more meaningful and effective, this practice should be discontinued and untied funds may be made available to PRIs through state budget. But instead of making this demand, the members of Panchayat bodies, particularly at the district and intermediate levels, have started demanding similar discretionary funds at their disposal. Another development is the reported decision of the government of Madhya Pradesh to give a discretionary fund of Rs. 50,000 to tahsildars when reports came about starvation/malnutrition deaths in some districts. This completely negates the intent to strengthen Panchayats to address such local needs. Panchayats too should not only be strengthened but also made accountable, instead the tendency is to look for alternative bodies, functionaries, etc.

Janmabhoomi Programme in Andhra Pradesh is another programme, which undermines the intention of 73rd Amendment to strengthen three-tier Panchayat structure for all planning and development and as institutions of self-government. Ostensibly, the programmes like Janmabhoomi are started for larger people's participation but when the Panchayat structure is in the whole country and in every village, taluka and district, the alternative structure of 'janmabhoomi' is questionable.

The state government launched this new programme on

1 January 1997 to promote participatory planning and development in rural areas. The programme incorporated the ongoing *prajala vaddaku palana* (administration on the door step) and the *shramdan* (voluntary labour) schemes. However, in bypassing the elected rural local bodies of Gram Panchayats, Mandal Parishads and Zila Parishads, this new programme has proved to be no different from the various special schemes and projects of the union and state governments for rural development and the MPs and MLAs Area Development Scheme. It, therefore, violates the spirit, if not the letter, of the 73rd Constitutional Amendment which gives a pivotal place to these bodies in planning and implementing programmes of economic and social development in the villages (Hargopal: 2000, p. 58)

Janmabhoomi programme has come as a big blow to the panchayats. "Andhra is a company, people are shareholders and the Chief Minister the General Manager" is the motto of the Janmabhoomi programme launched on 1 January 1997, based on the South Korean programme of development and experience: *Saemaul Undong* (New Community Movement). During the nine rounds of the Janmabhoomi, the state government had earmarked Rs. 1521.89 crore. The government share works out to be Rs. 975.95 crore. The state funds have been diverted from the allocations for central schemes such as Employment Assurance Scheme, Rural Water Supply Scheme, Jawahar Rozgar Yojna, Integrated Tribal Development Agency, DPEP, National Slum Development Programme, etc. The norms prescribed for the utilization of these funds are breached. Under the 10th round, funds are being used from health, medical and family welfare, women development and child welfare, rural development, labour development, labour, education, youth welfare, sports, municipal administration, animal husbandry, agriculture, horticulture and sericulture departments. Sweeping powers are given to the "nodal officers". A study by the National Institute of Rural Development (NIRD), Hyderabad, concludes:

> "The participation of members of Panchayati Raj bodies belonging to various political parties other than ruling party has been missing in this programme. It has sidetracked the Panchayati Raj institutions and other local bodies by

> maintaining parallel system of administration by according more importance to MLAs and other politicians" (ISS: 2000, p. 17).

This programme is coordinated by the Planning Department. Initially, the PRIs were kept out of its implementation. But later due to practical as well as political compulsions, the Sarpanchs, the Mandal Parishad Presidents and the Zila Parishad Chairmen have been involved in its implementation. For selection of works under this scheme, only elected representatives of PRIs at all the three levels have been involved now but it still remains a programme outside the domain of the PRIs as such.

Similarly, in a number of programmes started at the central level, separate institutional structures are devised as user groups of watersheds, joint forest management committees, and village education committees and so on instead of entrusting the programmes to PRIs. Early in 1999, Madhya Pradesh introduced the District Government consisting of the minister from the state government, district collector, MLAs, MPs from the area and the Zila Panchayat representatives. Wide powers have been conferred on the district government. The Collector would virtually be the chief executive of the district government gaining power immensely. All this has been done by making use of Article 243 ZD for the creation of the District Planning Committee. The title of District Government should have been conferred on a decentralized democratic body such as the Zila Panchayat, for the ZP is a body elected by the people in the district. Bypassing the Zila Panchayat, Madhya Pradesh now has a non-elected District Government. It has two implications: (1) Zila Panchayat President's status and position have been reduced and the ZP has become second to the so-called district government, (2) A clear parallel structure has been created through the district government, which is not a constitutional body. It will have far-reaching consequences for the development of Panchayati Raj system, and other states may follow the Madhya Pradesh example to sabotage the powers of local self-governments (ISS: 2000).

Madhya Pradesh has also introduced what it calls the Gram Swaraj with an amendment to the state Panchayati Raj Act in January 2001. Even the name of the state law has been changed from the Madhya Pradesh Panchayati Raj Act to Madhya Pradesh Panchayati Raj and Gram Swaraj Act. Gram Sabha will now be for every village, which has been recommended even at the national level, so that people can meet in their own village but this amendment includes setting up of eight committees of Gram Sabha other than the elected Gram Panchayat. These are Gram Vikas (village development) Samiti, Sarvajanik Sampada (common properties) Samiti, Krishi (agriculture), Swasthaya (health), Gram Raksha (village security), Adho Sanrachna (infrastructure), Shiksha (education), Sarvajanik Nyaya (social justice). Each consists of members from eight to twelve in number. The presidents of these committees have to be elected for one year and they will be on rotation from SC/ST/OBC/ General and women.

The Gram Vikas Samiti consists of all the presidents of the seven committees and Sarpanch would be its president. There will be a Gram Kosh, consisting of Anna Kosh, Shram Kosh, Vastu Kosh and Nagar Kosh to be operated by the Gram Vikas Samiti. In practice, one does not find these multiple 'Kosh' in the villages. A treasurer has to be appointed or selected separately. The joint signature of the treasurer and the secretary (now changed to Sarpanch) will be needed to withdraw amounts from the Gram Kosh. The Gram Panchayats have to transfer to these committees all the funds made available by the central or state government and its own funds The powers of taxation or raising resources etc., which were indicated against the Panchayats in the original law, are now shown against the Gram Sabha. Appeal against the Gram Sabha's decision is done to an appeal committee consisting of SDO (Revenue), Janpad Panchayat President and Janpad Panchayat Member of the area. Thus, in the name of Gram Sabha new standing committees have been introduced outside the Gram Panchayats and given all powers and resources. These committees effectively undermine the capacity and authority of the Gram Panchayats and particularly of the Gram Panchayat presidents.

The law also provides that no meeting of the committee can take place if it does not have the quorum. A review of the recent reports of the Gram Sabha meetings for Gram Swaraj and constitution of standing committees and of setting up of Gram Kosh shows that even by the end of the year 2001-2002, these standing committees have been constituted in 76 per cent places and Gram Kosh set up in 57 per cent of the places. In some districts, particularly in the western region, like Ujjain, Mandsaur, Shajapur, Rajgarh, Bhind (32 per cent) and Rewa, only 35 per cent to 38 per cent Gram Sabhas had constituted these committees. In a number of places where the Sarpanch is from the reserved category or a woman, the treasurer and other chairpersons are mainly men from non-reserved category.

By now the M.P experiment of Gram Swaraj, started in 2000, has shown some of the expected implications. In a number of villages, there were conflicts and clashes in the elections to these bodies particularly of the treasurer who has the authority in utilisation of all the funds given to the Gram Panchayat but who is outside the Gram Panchayat and has no responsibility for the progress of works etc. in the Gram Panchayat area. So he becomes the counter -force to the village Panchayat Sarpanch who is duly elected by the whole of the Panchayat area, which may have one or more villages. An interesting implication of this experiment is that while the 1996 law extending Panchayat provisions to the Schedule V Areas mandated that all heads of village Panchayats, block Panchayats and district Panchayats have to be tribals, these bodies need not have only tribals and therefore in a number of cases while the village Panchayat head is a tribal man or a tribal woman, these bodies are headed by non-tribal men thereby effectively bringing persons in position who were out due to the 1996 law and/or by the reservations for STs and for women.

The experiment is ostensibly made for increasing the authority and primacy of the Gram Sabha. The committees are supposed to be elected by the Gram Sabha but they effectively undermine any authority and work to be done by the Gram Panchayat. The funds given to the Gram Panchayats by the central or state government or coming from their own resources have to be given to these committees which have been made for specific subjects like education, social justice, construction, etc. The chairpersons of these committees are to be elected every year and hence ensure that neither Panchayat leadership nor the leadership in these committees have any chance of developing or showing their performance.

EMERGING TRENDS AND CHALLENGES

In most of the state Panchayat laws, the state government can cancel or suspend any resolution of the panchayat at any level if, in its opinion, any such resolution abuses the provisions of any Act. The government also has powers to dissolve Panchayats and dismiss PRI heads at all the three levels. Thus, the state Panchayat Acts give considerable powers to the government to control the Panchayati Raj bodies. Besides, the state Panchayat laws seem to place reliance more on the executive officers than the political heads of the panchayat bodies for proper functioning of the latter.

The XI Schedule added by the 73rd Amendment was to serve as a guide, so that the respective state legislatures could decide which among the different functions or sub-functions of the subjects listed in this Schedule could be statutorily transferred to the PRIs. Once such transfer was made, the PRIs would have absolute authority to deal with them without reference to the state government. In other words, the Constitution intended transfer of authority and responsibility over a set of functions or sub-functions from the state government to the PRIs. Such transfer implies that both financial and administrative resources necessary for discharge of the transferred functions should also be devolved to the Panchayats. But there is a contradiction in the scheme of the state Acts. It admits that Panchayat is an institution of self-government, but fails to carve out independent jurisdiction for the PRIs, subject to the mandatory provisions of the Constitution in respect of election, structure, reservation of seats and position of chairpersons etc. Conceptually, these institutions remain as before merely statutory authorities without any independent jurisdiction over a set of governmental functions. The State Panchayat Acts seem to have no idea of devolution instead of decentralisation, which is intended by the Constitution.

Thus, the post-73rd Amendment evolution of the Panchayati Raj institutions in the states so far deviates from the vision of this Amendment as much as they continue to be conceived not as institutions of self-government but as implementing subordinate agencies of the state government. Hence, decentralisation that has taken place in the states has, by and large, been in the nature of deconcentration of government's activities and not devolution of authority and functions. The conformity Acts in the wake of the Amendment to meet its mandatory requirements of the states did not alter the character of Panchayats in terms of Article 243 G read with the XI Schedule. In practice also, they did little to reduce the agency functions of Panchayats and expand their autonomous jurisdiction. The Panchayats have continued to function as the implementing agencies for the state government's schemes most of which are centrally-sponsored poverty alleviation schemes. Untied funding for Panchayats is practically an unknown concept to most of the state governments. In fact, even the "untied funds" earlier made available in some of the states to the district planning boards under the Planning Commission's insistence for district level planning have been withdrawn for making them available as discretionary funds to ministers and members of state legislative assemblies. This is one of the major reasons why no Panchayat even in West Bengal fulfils the constitutional mandate of preparing area plans for economic development and social justice, even though the State Panchayat Act confers this responsibility on them.

Lack of clarity about the role of Panchayats as envisioned in the 73rd Amendment becomes pronounced when one sees parallel institutions set up in areas which legitimately belong to the Panchayati Raj institutions. Even though primary education is a subject listed in the XI Schedule, the Panchayats have not been allowed to retain any control over the mainstream primary education system even in West Bengal where a separate institution called District Primary Education Council has been created to run the primary schools.

Our brief overview of the action taken to implement the mandate of the 73rd Amendment and the 1996 law extending Panchayat provisions to the Schedule V areas shows that while mandatory provisions have been complied with, there are still some deviations primarily from the spirit of these enactments but also some from the letter of the enactments too which need to be corrected without waiting for litigation and court decisions. Most important are the deviations from the spirit of these amendments. The development programmes and funds for rural areas need to be squarely entrusted to the Panchayat institutions for planning and implementation according to local aspirations and requirements. The increasing practice of creating parallel structures for implementation of development programmes and for people's participation must be stopped and any new mechanisms should be created only within the structure of the Panchayats at the three levels and not outside even if ostensibly created in the name of Gram Sabha or people's participation. Any problems in the working of the Panchayats need to be corrected by appropriate training, exposure and orientation, instead of countering them by external outside structures and institutions.

Special chapters seen in most of the state Panchayat laws which provide for control and other provisions which give extensive powers to the state government to supersede panchayat institutions and to take action against their elected representatives should be changed as these are really continuation of the conception of Panchayats in the colonial period when the Panchayats were created from the top, were quite often optional institutions and were to be strictly controlled. Any control should be through independent institutions and authorities like the State Election Commission or new authorities which can be evolved as tribunals or commissions and not with the state governments and their subordinate authorities so that requisite corrective steps are taken where necessary without being influenced by the state politics.

At present, the Central and State Government grants are given to Panchayats with specific conditions and guidelines. These are all tied grants giving no space for Panchayats to use these grants based on the locally identified needs of the Gram Sabha area. This needs to be changed and most of the funds should be given as untied funds. Funds allotted to Members of Parliament and Members of the Legislative Assembly should be used only as part of the planning process from below by the district Panchayats and Panchayats at the village and intermediate levels.

It would be desirable for Local Self-Government Institutions to have their own officers and staff. They should have powers of appointment, transfer and disciplinary action about their staff, especially in regard to institutions catering to the fulfilment of basic needs in the villages. The control and decision on usage and regeneration with regard to all common lands and natural resources/common property resources and waterbodies should be vested with the village Panchayats. Every village Panchayat should mandatorily maintain village maps, details of the village common resources, etc. All recommendations with regard to reclassification of village maps and land-use management and changes in uses of common property resources, natural, resources, etc., must be entrusted with Panchayats after adoption by the Gram Sabha.

Constitution of a State Development Council of Panchayat Institutions in each state will be useful to propose and deliberate on policy directions and evaluate the functioning of rural local government bodies. It should meet at least twice a year. To sum up. If we look at the omissions and deficiencies in implementation of the provisions of 73rd Amendment, we see that there has been a more mechanical compliance than a display of real commitment to give power to people's institutions at the grassroots. There is an unspoken lack of confidence in the abilities of the local people to handle their affairs. There is reluctance to leave space to people to learn from their initial mistakes and to become stronger in addressing their local needs with resources and powers available with them. Another aspect is competition between different levels of the polity to keep control and power over allocation of resources for addressing different needs. This accounts for the trend to seek discretionary funds for individual elected persons at different levels, instead of working through the statutorily mandated and elected institutions with participation and negotiation of all concerned so that priorities for use of resources for different needs can be decided collectively. In a way, it is also a carryover of feudal and patriarchal mindset which does not permit the earlier marginalized groups and women to be in decision-making roles despite the constitutional mandate and everyone at least speaking in support of decentralization, grassroots democracy, people's participation, etc. Hence, we find that the legislative and executive action taken in even in those states who swear by their commitment to decentralization, devolution and Gandhi's Gram Swaraj falls short of the real philosophy of the 73rd Amendment. The measures like two child norm, parallel committees and structures outside the constitutionally mandated Gram Panchayats have already shown their adverse, unequal impact on women and weaker sections and assertion and power of those who were to give way to share political power at the grassroots with the earlier politico-socially marginalized groups. Grassroots democracy needs content of responsibilities, resources and powers and a reasonable continuity and guarantee in exercise of those powers to show any impact. It is time to act to strengthen the PRIs and for effective inclusion and participation of these sections to meet the expectations and intent of the historic Amendment of 1992 by countering practices consciously or unintentionally influenced by feudal and patriarchal powers.

References

Hargopal, G., G. Sudarshanam (2000): Andhra Pradesh – in *ISS: Status of Panchayat Raj in the States and UTs of India*.

Institute of Social Studies, ISS (2000): *Status of Panchayati Raj in the State and Union Territories of India 2000: ISS 2000*.

Mahila Chetna Manch (MCM) (2003): Panchayati Raj and the 'Two Child Norm', Implications and Consequences, A summary of the Preliminary Findings of Exploratory studies in Andhra Pradesh, Haryana, Madhya Pradesh, Orissa and Rajasthan – Mahila Chetna Manch, Bhopal, January 2003.

Shastry, K.R. (1999): Panchayats Raj in Andhra Pradesh: Recent Developments – *Kurukshetra*, April 1999.

6

Convergence of Programmes by Empowering the Self-Help Groups and Panchayati Raj Institutions[1]

*D. Bandyopadhyay**, *B.N. Yugandhar**
and *Amitava Mukherjee**

I. INTRODUCTION

Andhra Pradesh is unique among the Indian states in having seven to ten community-based organizations in the nature of self-help groups covering seven to ten activities like education, water use, thrift, watershed, youth development, etc., in every village. In a district, there are approximately 20,000 to 25,000 such groups. Two of these groups are statutory in character and the others are community-based organizations. All groups are not equally vibrant and effective, as is true of any class of groups. However, there is no denying the fact that nowhere in India there is as much of mobilization of interest groups, particularly women, as in Andhra Pradesh. These groups, given some inputs of capacity building and skill, could be a formidable social force and pressure lobby in promoting development in the state through promoting and protecting their respective interests and weal.

These self-help groups, however, interface with a large number of government and elected institutions at the grass-

---

1. Originally published in Economic and Political Weekely, Mumbai.

*(Members, Poverty Eradication Mission, Government of Andhra Pradesh)

roots level, particularly the Panchayati Raj Institutions. The efficacy of these self-help groups (SHGs) would be considerably enhanced if a symbiosis could be worked out between the SHGs and the Panchayati Raj Institutions. The key to this is to integrate these existing groups with the democratically elected and empowered Panchayats when the requisite devolution of powers, functions and authority to them takes place. Because the space for development administration and political processes at the sub-district levels are limited now, the PRIs are competing with the SHGs for such space. And this unhealthy competition has been further exacerbated by the niggardly delegation of powers and functions to the PRIs. Because the PRIs have insufficient understanding of the constructive role that the SHGs can play in upliftment of the masses, they are unable to configure a working relationship with the SHGs. Thus, the possibility that ultimately the PRIs could try to stifle or suppress these SHGs, perhaps as threats to their own existence, cannot be ruled out. If it happens, it would be a tragedy. People's initiatives blossomed into such self-help groups would get repressed and that would ultimately reduce the effectiveness of PRIs as they would have no pressure lobby to interact with. There is an urgent need to work out mechanisms/systems that will allow the SHGs and the PRIs to work at tandem and establish a system of reinforcing each other's work.

II. THE RATIONALE OF BUILDING LINKAGE BETWEEN PRIs AND SHGs

Establishing a system through which the SHGs and the PRIs interface efficiently, is eminently possible because by nature and mandate both these institutions have the same objective, viz., of ushering people-centred development and through it to empower the disempowered.

Constitutionally mandated three-tier Panchayat institutions symbolize representative governance at the district level and below. To be potent and effective such bodies must respond to the needs and sensitivities of different interest groups. But unless there is some compelling force, instead of being responsive, they might turn out to be sterile elected bureaucracy as it has happened in some states. To enhance these responsiveness, accountability and transparency, there should be an institutional and functional linkage with these S.H.G.

SHGs and Gram Panchayats

The Conformity Act establishing panchayats in Andhra Pradesh following the 73rd (and 74th) Constitution Amendments, viz., Andhra Pradesh Panchayati Raj Act 1994, provides for six functional standing committees at the Gram Panchayat (GP) level. The seven to ten self-help groups operating at the village level also represent more or less the same or similar types of activities. The Gram Sabhas shall co-opt one or more representatives of the SHGs into the respective Standing Committees of the Gram Panchayat. These co-opted members would fully participate in the proceedings of the Standing Committees, except voting. The members of the SHGs on the Standing Committees would act as pressure groups and lobby in these committees and since they would be representing significant segments of the constituents, it would be difficult for the GPs to ignore their views and demands. The scheme outlined here is akin to what was adopted in a scheme under the Third Republic in France, called *cumul des mandas*, where mayors of communes and others elected to local offices were also elected to legislative offices, which ensured that the legislature functioned under checks provided by local interest (Schmidt, 1990).

It is clarified here that in cases where the Standing Committees have been established habitation-wise, because of the large size of some of the Gram Panchayats, the scheme of representation of the SHGs will be carried out habitation-wise.

After having established a functional relationship with GPs, these SHGs can act as both implementing and monitoring agencies of the relevant schemes and programmes. Since GPs would have to function under the constant watch and vigil of the SHGs, the GPs will have to discharge their duties and obligation more effectively, frugally and sincerely to the satisfaction of the villagers. By providing for this measure of co-option of SHGs into the Standing Committees of the GPs , it is possible for the state government to bring out radical qualitative change in the operational efficiency of the GPs.

The selection of the representatives of SHGs to be co-opted to the respective Standing Committees at the GP level will be through the open Gram Sabha meeting. There need not be any formal election. Selection may take place through consensus or by show of hands. However, if consensus building is not possible, one should not shy away from formal elections as well. Co-option of members from the SHGs into the Standing Committees by consensus or election in open Gram Sabha meeting would give these co-opted members considerable clout of popular acceptance and mandate, which the GPs usually cannot disregard.

SHGs and Mandal Level Panchayats: Panchayat Samiti

At the Mandal Praja Parishad, members of the SHGs will also be co-opted to the Standing Committees of the Mandal Praja Parishads. The process of co-option of SHG members as members of the Standing Committees at the Mandal level will be slightly different but along similar lines. Members from the SHGs will be co-opted to the Mandal level Standing Committees from amongst the co-opted members of Standing Committees of the Gram Panchayats, for each activity groups. For example, if there are 20 GPs in a Mandal, and in each Standing Committee of each GP, of say watershed, there are two co-opted members, then would be total of 40 co-opted members of watershed committees in the Gram Panchayats. At the Mandal level, co-option to the Watershed Standing Committee would be made from amongst these 40 members of watershed committees at the Gram Panchayats. This will be done through an open meeting to the whole Mandal Praja Parishads.

SHGs and District Level Panchayats: Zila Parishads

In a similar manner, co-option from members of the SHGs should be made to the Standing Committees of the Zila Parishads. Members from the SHGs will be co-opted to the Zila Parishad level Standing Committees from amongst the co-opted members of Standing Committees of the Mandal Praja Parishads, for each activity groups. For example, if there are 10 Mandal level Standing Committees in a Mandal, and in each Standing Committee of each Panchayat Samiti, of say watershed, there are two co-opted members, then would be total of 20 co-opted members of watershed committees in the Mandal Praja Parishads. At the Zila Parishad level, co-option to the relevant standing committee would be made from amongst these 20 members. This will be done through an open meeting to the Zila Parishad.

This process of co-option to the Standing Committees at the GPs, MPs and ZPs would provide an organic linkage between the SHGs at the habitation/village level and the three-tier PRIs, which would be mutually beneficial.

The symbiotic relationship between the SHGs and the PRIs is shown in Diagram 6.1.

While at the GP level, SHGs could be implementing, monitoring and evaluating agencies, apart from acting as pressure groups and lobbies, at the MP and ZP levels they would primarily act as lobby to provide feedback from habitation/village level realities to the Panchayat Samitis and Zila Parishad and act as watchdogs to promote and protect their own interest.

At the village level, there are organizations like water users' organization and education committees, which are statutory bodies. Relevant laws governing these organizations should be amended to align them within the overall fold of the Panchayats.

III. ISSUES OF CONVERGENCE

The success of the benefits, Flowing from attaining the symbiosis envisaged between the SHGs and the PRIs, will depend to a large extent on three elements:

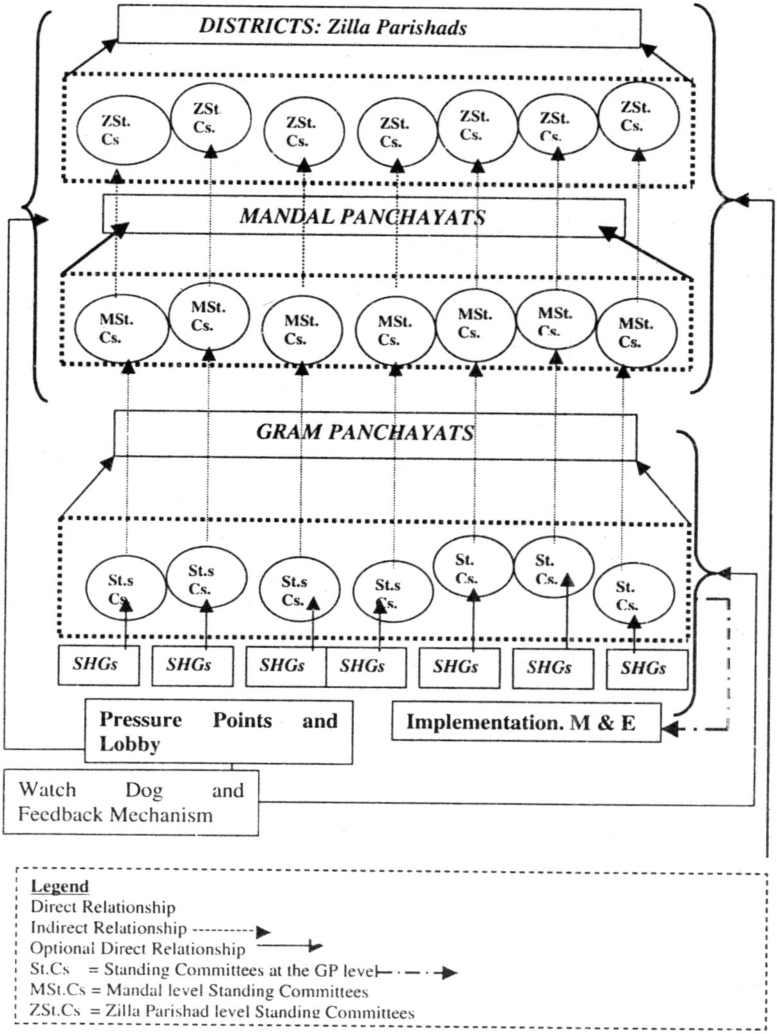

Diagram 6.1: Diagrammatic Representation of the Proposed Relationship between Self-help Groups and Panchayati Raj Institutions in Andhra Pradesh

(a) Strengthening of the Panchayati Raj Institutions themselves. The rationale for this is too obvious to be laboured here. Suffice it to say that weak institutions cannot deliver the goods and procrastinating constitutionally mandated elected institutions are breeding grounds for discontent and discord resulting in adverse political fall out.

(b) Affecting convergence of development programmes and initiatives being implemented in the state by different agencies and line departments. There is total compartmentalization of functions, not infrequently similar, between agencies and departments so that several departments engaged in identical activities under similar circumstances achieve dissimilar results. There is wastage of resources. There are delays in implementation, duplication of work and organizational friction.

(c) Building the capacity of the self-help groups. Community-based institutions have the communal wisdom and possess time-tested knowledge handed down from one generation to the other as bequest but they do not always have the technology of putting such wisdom and knowledge to generate self sustaining development along the warranted path.

The need to address these three issues cannot be over-emphasized to which we shall presently turn.

IV. MEASURES FOR STRENGTHENING PRIs

The Government of Andhra Pradesh has taken steps to transfer subjects mentioned in the Eleventh Schedule of the Constitution to all the tiers of PRIs, through Government Orders. In reality, though this decentralization is indicative of a move in the right direction, the quantum of true decentralization in terms of transfer of functions, functionaries and finances have been miserly and inadequate. According to the Report of the Task Force on Devolution of Powers and Functions upon PRIs,

Ministry of Rural Development, Government of India, Andhra Pradesh transferred functions in respect of 13 subjects, funds for 5 subjects and functionaries for only two (Annexure III, p. 53). For the decentralization of powers and authority to the PRIs to be effective and meaningful as envisioned by the letter and spirit of the Constitution, it is imperative that decentralization must include, but not restricted to, the delegation of administrative, fiscal and sectoral responsibilities to PRIs. We repeat even at the cost of suffering the stricture of being repetitive, that no scheme of decentralization would be effective unless it is accompanied by the delegation of functions, functionaries and finances.

Coordination of development departments and dynamic development decision making is an essential requisite for poverty reduction and universalisation of access to basic amenities such as elementary education, primary healthcare, eradication of communicable diseases, sanitation and public distribution system. Strengthening PRIs with authority, powers and functionaries over these and such other sectoral activities and enhancing their capabilities for district and local level planning is an important stage in this direction. The Danish experiment at empowering in the early 1970s the local level authorities by creating the present two-tier structure of "Kommune" and AMT (country administration) and delegating suitable functions to them, helped the local level governments to be freed from unnecessary controls and deliver the basic services efficiently (Etherington and Paddon, 1991) while at once strengthen democracy.

Improved governance, greater accountability and transparency together with the convergence and better co-ordination in these sectors (to which we will revert later in this chapter) is also critical to the realization of objectives mentioned in the Vision 2020 document, especially in the areas of poverty reduction and social development. The involvement of Panchayati Raj Institutions, in addition to these advantages, would also unleash the latent creativity and productivity of the community in manifold directions.

Government of Andhra Pradesh has done several exercises

for identifying programmes and projects for transfer to PRIs. Reports of several expert groups are also available on this subject. The best practices followed in other states under similar circumstances have also been studied and highlighted from time to time. Keeping all these in view and considering the specific challenges encountered by Andhra Pradesh at this juncture, activity mapping among the 3 tiers of Panchayati Raj Institutions and transfer of functions, funds and functionaries based on these activities to each tier is not only possible, but is urgently desired. Care has to be taken in transferring of functions, funds and functionaries, for these have to be informed by the principle of subsidiary, i.e., functions, funds and functionaries are to be transferred to the level at which these functions can be best performed.

We are of the view that development activities in social sectors must be given high priority, particularly so for directly targeting poverty reduction efforts. These activities can succeed only when the involvement of people in general and of representative and participatory democratic institutions in particular is firmly secured.

We feel that 29 subjects in Eleventh Schedule of the Constitution should be divided into activities and *inter-se* division of these activities among the 3 tiers of Panchayati Raj Institutions has to be notified and made part of the Conformity Act. We are confident when these are further analyzed with reference to specific programmes and schemes as enumerated in the state budget, the exercise of decentralization will be more meaningful. These suggestions are in conformity with the recent recommendations adopted by the Ministers in-charge of Panchayati Raj Institutions at a conference held in New Delhi in the month of October 2001.

Taking an integrated view, it is desirable that instead of leaving the individual departments in the Government of Andhra Pradesh to decide upon the transfer of activities and related functions, functionaries and finances to the PRIs, all the details pertaining to such transfer among 3 tiers of Panchayati Raj Institutions may be considered holistically. Comprehensive statutory provisions regarding this transfer may be enjoined as rules to Andhra Pradesh Panchayati Raj

Act 1994. This would enable speedy consideration of this matter and integrated view of the decentralization process. Further, it is imperative that the division of functions, functionaries and finances suggested by us pertaining to the 19 subjects as well as the *inter-se* distribution of such functions, functionaries and finances, between the 3 tiers of Panchayat Raj may be incorporated in full, in the Schedules annexed to the Andhra Pradesh Panchayati Raj Act 1994.

The scheme of decentralization recommended by us is amenable for monitoring, review and evaluation of performance parameters on which the process of decentralization in Andhra Pradesh can be succeeded. Their performance indicators would be:

(a) The percentage of planned funds channelized through Panchayati Raj institutions;
(b) The amount of untied funds made available to these bodies;
(c) The quality of the plans and the programmes formulated and implemented by PRIs;
(d) The extra budgetary resources raised by Panchayati Raj bodies through "shramdan" and other contributions to enhance the quality and implementation of their plans and programmes; and
(e) Innovative measures taken by the PRIs to improve the quality of planning and implementation in areas of natural resource management, human resource development and poverty reduction.

V. AFFECTING CONVERGENCE

Convergence of programmes and development initiatives has been an issue that has agitated the development administration in the state for considerable length of time. The state of convergence is best illustrated by Diagram 6.2. Though the issue of convergence seems intractable, there are models and mechanisms of convergence available in the state and in the country, which have unfortunately fallen into disuse. It is necessary to restore those mechanisms and indeed it has

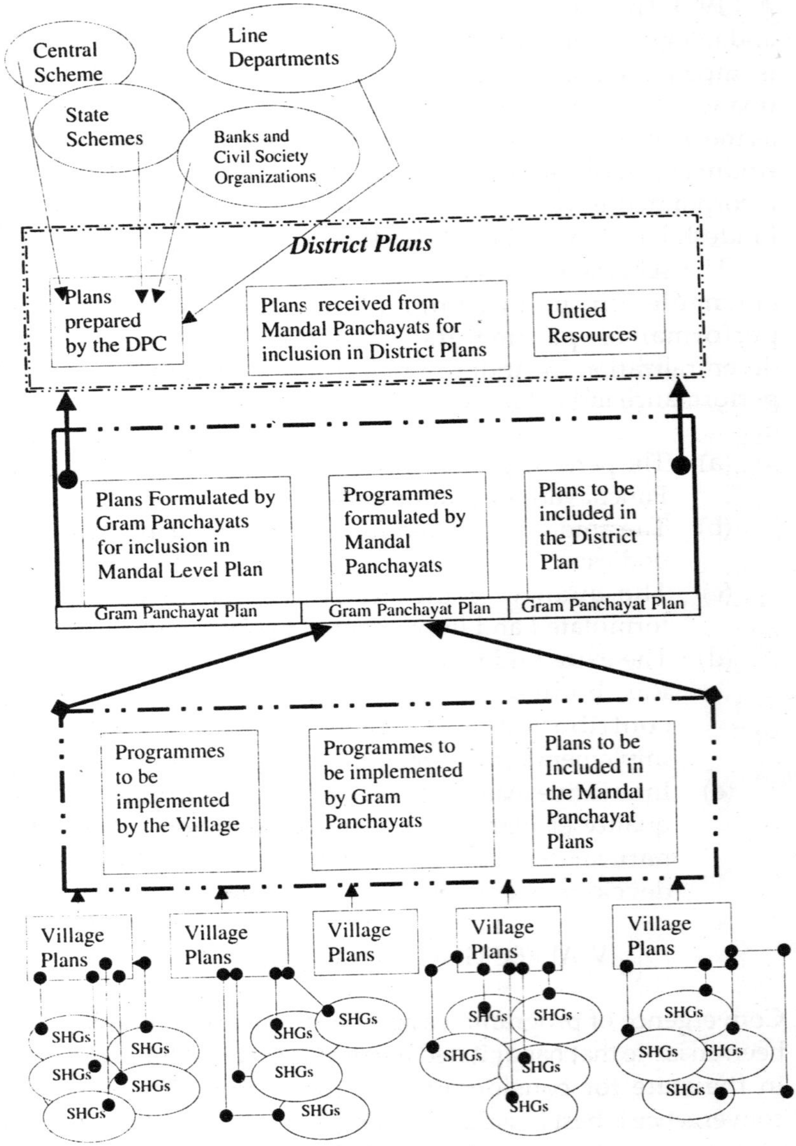

Diagram 6.2: A Suggested Planning System

become much simpler to do so now than ever before as enabling constitutional provisions are in place within the ambit of Article 243G.

Convergence has to be tackled at two levels:

(a) Strengthening the mechanisms for planning and allocation of resources, at the district and the sub-district levels, for carrying out development programmes, across sectors by different agencies and departments; and
(b) Implementation of development programmes.

For strengthening the mechanism for planning and allocation of resources at the district and the sub-district levels, the measures that would bear results on a long term basis have to be on two planes: one, on the *philosophy* of planning, and two, on the *engineering* of planning. Let us deal with these issues in turn.

First, on the *philosophy* of planning the state must demonstrate its acceptance of the concept that for development and poverty alleviation to be long lasting, planning processes and systems must revolve around people-centred development. People have to be looked as the fundamental resource and not as problems for whom planning is devised. The state must demonstrate the acceptance of the philosophy

- that people know their problems best,
- that people have solutions to solve their problems through use of local knowledge, local resources and indigenous technology,
- that people have the capacity and capability to plan to solve their problems best, especially so in contemporaneous Andhra Pradesh where large number of community-based organizations (in the nature of SHGs) are operating which have contributed to the empowerment of the people, and
- that the role of the state and its agencies has to that of a facilitator (which includes building technical capability of the people) of the process where people prepare and implement plans for their development.

Endorsement of such a philosophy will require considerable change in the outlook and attitude of the development administration in the state. While these concepts may look simply and intuitively appealing to common sense, operationalizing them will require considerable state effort, political will and re-orientation of bureaucratic thinking.

This brings us to the **second issue**. On the ***engineering of planning***, the letter and spirit of the 73rd Constitution Amendment, the underlying logic of decentralization and making people-centred development a reality, can be taken to its logical end by putting in systems, processes, structures and institutions which will promote people-centred plan. The following steps are urgently required:

(a) The Structure

The *District Planning Committees* as enjoined in Article 243ZD of the Constitution should be so constituted that one-fifth of the members be from amongst:

- The Collector,
- PD, DRDAs,
- Heads of Departments at the District Level,
- Development NGOs, Lead Bank Manager,
- Manager, NABARD, and
- Such other local technical experts that may be available.

With the President/Chairperson of ZP as the Chairperson, these Committees will be apolitical and purely technical in nature.

The *Mandal Level Planning Committees* may be constituted with the President of the Panchayat Samiti, Mandal Development Officer, key officers from the line departments and such other technical people who may be available at the Mandal Level.

At the Gram Panchayat Level, Panchayat Planning Committees are to be constituted with one representative from each of the self-help groups, the village school teacher (if available) and the Panches.

(b) The Process to be Mandated

The process of planning at the district and sub-district levels will essentially be bottom up approach. The steps involved in this approach shall be as follows:

Step-1: Village Level Plan

Village level plans will be prepared using the participatory-based methods. These methods will include, but not restricted to, participatory poverty assessment, participatory resource mapping, force field analysis, livelihood analysis, seasonal calendars, etc., all of which have been documented and used in different parts of the world (Mukherjee, 2001) and in India, especially in Kerala (Chattopadhyay *et at.*, 2000; Mukherjee, 1995).

In case the villages have households exceeding 100, the village may be divided into several localities (habitation) and plans prepared for each habitation and then aggregated and harmonized at the village level. These village level plans will be prepared with the help of the SHGs.

Step-2: Gram Panchayat Plans

Once the village plans are prepared, Gram Panchayat planning will be undertaken. The Gram Panchayat Planning basically will have four elements:

(a) A systematic collection and collation of plans in respect of all the villages under the Gram Panchayat.

(b) The Gram Panchayat will then separate plans, schemes or programmes which involve more than one village from plans, schemes or programmes, which can be implemented in individual villages. The former should be examined and included in the Gram Panchayat Plan and the latter should be kept as Village Level Plans.

(c) The Gram Panchayat will then prepare a plan in respect of those sectors, which are to be implemented at the Gram Panchayat level on their own motion or upon the delegated authority to do so by the state government. It will include in such a Plan the plans schemes and programmes, which the village plans have generated for the Gram Panchayat as stated above.

(d) Those plans, schemes or programmes, which have been prepared for the Gram Panchayat as a whole but which cannot be taken up for implementation at the Panchayat level as they involve more than one Gram Panchayat, must be identified. These must be mentioned in the Gram Panchayat Plan as the schemes to be included while preparing the Mandal level Plans.

Step-3

The Gram Panchayat Plans will be approved in the Gram Sabha.

Step-4: Plans for Mandals

Plans for Mandals will then be prepared. Except for some specific characteristics of the Gram Panchayat Plans, by and large, the steps and methodology applicable for village plan will also apply to Mandal Panchayat Plan preparation.

It is critical that the format in which the Mandal Panchayat, Gram Panchayat Plans and the village plans are to be prepared be the same so that the integration of the village plan with the plans of the three tiers of the Panchayati Raj Institutions becomes easy.

The state government will have to spell out the powers and jurisdiction of the Mandal Praja Parishads (Mandal level Panchayats) in respect of planning. In village planning and Gram Panchayat planning, the Mandal Level Planning Committee will have to be vested with the authority to create planning culture whereby plans of the lower tiers (Gram Panchayat and village level) will be correctly prepared and integrated with the Mandal Level Plans.

The critical roles of Mandal Parishad in the planning process are at *Appendix-A*.

Step-5: District Plan

Preparation of the district plans: Once Mandal plans are prepared, they are forwarded to the Zila Parishad for integration into the district plan.

The Zila Parishad will prepare the district plans. The Zila Parishad will prepare the district plan taking into account the demands of the line departments, the "District Sector Plans" received from the Mandal Praja Panchayats and the plans of the banks and NABARD.

Step-6: Financing Sectors

Division of Plans: The plans prepared for the villages and the Gram Panchayats will have to focus on what can be achieved in the short run first. The village plans and the Gram Panchayat plans will provide all the required interventions in the **4** sectors, namely, *People's Sector, Bank Sector, Government Sector and Combined Sector.*

The People's Sector will contain all development interventions which the people can do themselves. For example, maintenance of community tanks, village path or preservation of sacred groves. The Bank Sector will include development interventions which is possible by availing credit from the bank, which could include creation of income generating assets, livestock, etc.

The Government Sector will include activities or projects which can be executed by government funding. This could include construction of roads, bridges, check dams, infrastructure, running of schools, etc. The combined sector is a residual sector, where all development activities that require people's contribution, flow of credit and government financing as also private sector investment as appropriate. These could be in the nature of setting up an agro-processing unit.

Step-7: Time Element

Once the different plans, programmes and activities are

separated in terms of the *four sectors*, in step 6, time element has to be injected. All plans, programmes and activities will then have to be divided into separate groups depending upon the period over which they need to be implemented. A suggested way of classifying plans, programmes and activities, according the period during which they will be implemented, may be in terms of short term (1 to 2 years), medium term (2 to 5 years) and long term (5 years and beyond). For example, desilting of ponds, introduction of kitchen gardens and pasture/grassland development may be classified as schemes to be implemented in the *short term*. Similarly, pisciculture, sericulture, construction of roads, etc., may be classified as schemes to be implemented in the *medium term*.

VI. CONVERGENCE IN IMPLEMENTATION

While planning from below will ensure that convergence of programmes and plans take place, convergence of implementation will have to be ensured through convergence of implementation. This will be achieved by

(a) delegating functions, functionaries and finances to the different tiers of the Panchayati Raj Institutions on the principle of subsidiarity, and
(b) by separating the functional domain of the Panchayati Raj Institutions and development administration at the district and sub-district levels.

It is possible to achieve these by strengthening the Panchayati Raj Institutions to which we have discussed in Section V above and by setting clear limits of authority of the development functionaries, PRIs and elected members of the legislature. Overlapping areas of responsibilities, amongst other features, have been identified as one of the basic weaknesses of the current state of decentralization in India (Gaiha, 1997). This will help avoid wastage of effort and resources and help avoid mistakes made in this regard in India and in different parts of the world. For instance, in Italy local government is a maze of overlapping jurisdictions with mountain communities, metropolitan areas, local councils in some large urban communes and a variety of authorities with jurisdictions over particular issues (Spence, 1993 and Sananatonio, 1987). This has been one of the factors that have held back Italy from achieving faster economic growth.

VII. THE LESSONS FROM EXPERIENCE AND THE DIFFERENCE

There have been several experiments in this country and abroad in decentralization and development, which offer valuable lessons. The cases of West Bengal, Kerala and Karnataka in India, and of Spain, Italy and France in Europe are examples in point.

West Bengal attempted at empowering the Panchayati Raj Institutions by delegating substantial powers of planning (Misra and Sen, 1985) and authority on some of the items enjoined in the Eleventh Schedule to the Constitution. These measures, taken with other factors, have contributed significantly towards improving rural prosperity in the state and help a coalition government to sustain itself for nearly quarter of a century, imparting political stability, vital for social and economic development. The empowerment of the people in general has also contributed to strengthen grassroots democracy, as bedrock for stable government at the state level.

The experiments in Kerala have attracted considerable global attention. Empowering the Panchayats has helped in ushering people's campaign that culminated in completion of local development plans based on thorough process of bottom up approach, never before attempted in India and probably in the world (Harris, 2000). And it demonstrated the role that 'outsiders' (from the perspective of the bureaucracy and PRIs) in the nature of volunteers from organizations like Kerala Sahitya Parishad can play to make the effort such a success. The empowerment of the PRIs in terms of devolution of functions and clear earmarking of substantive financial resources (Thomas *et al.* 2000) have contributed to rapid social development in the state and significant economic progress.

The Government of Karnataka has also made significant

changes to empower the PRIs, particularly in the eighties, which had reaped benefits for the people, including efficiency in delivery of basic services. As early as 1983, prior even to the 73rd Constitutional Amendment, by the Zila Parishad etc. Act of 1983 transferred a wide range of functions for agriculture, rural industries to welfare of scheduled castes, scheduled tribes and backward classes to PRIs and contained provisions enabling the state government to delegate further powers and functions to PRIs. In exercise of the powers so vested in the government, in 1987 as many as 257 schemes covering important activities of over 20 line departments were transferred to Zila Parishad sector. Similarly, 89 Plan Schemes were transferred to Mandal Praja Parishads in the same order. Mandal Sector schemes were further split up into schemes which could be implemented by Mandals entirely on their own and schemes which were to be implemented by the Zila Parishads with Mandal Praja Parishads having the responsibility for planning, selection of beneficiaries, supervision and reporting (Government of Karnataka, 1997).

Having learnt from the foregoing success stories, this we recommend a scheme for convergence of programmes and strengthening participative organizations and constitutional democracy, which is a distinct improvement over other efforts. The reasons are not far to seek. Firstly, there is currently no other decentralization mechanism in place being pursued which brings about a symbiosis between participative organizations (SHGs) and constitutional democratic institutions (PRIs) on ongoing basis. The role to be performed by the SHGs in the Standing Committees and in the Planning Committees at the Gram Panchayat level will amply bear this out. Different states have Standing Committees at the Gram Panchayat level (such as the ones formed in Madhya Pradesh under section 7-A of The Madhya Pradesh Panchayat Raj Sanshodhan Adhiniyam 2001) but none have as yet integrated the SHGs with the Standing Committees. Secondly, the scheme of integrating the SHGs and PRIs will bring about more accountability in the stakeholders and increase the transparency in the operation of the different development actors at the district and sub-district levels, particularly the latter. Thirdly, the fact that the planning and implementation of the development programmes will be built on the bedrock of needs and priorities articulated by a large number of self-help groups, will impart greater community ownership to development programmes. This in the last analysis will ensure significant cut in wastage and leakage. Fourthly, the mechanism suggested by us will be far more amenable to social auditing and development of "social capital" than any scheme of decentralization currently operational in India. This scheme of decentralization will have an in-built mechanism of checks and balances between the participatory organizations and the democratic institutions. Finally, the process will help in restoring the faith of the people in the constitutional set-up and provide a mechanism to bring the people out of the culture of silence or violence into which they have been (often unwillingly) trapped. Thus, the formation and buttressing of psychological capital will be substantive.

In fine, while better planning of development programmes and better implementation of programmes will increase the physical and financial capital, the integration of participative organizations with the democratic institutions along with the bottom up planning and people-centred implementation, the development plans outlined by us will lead to social and psychological capital. The diagram 6.2 encapsulates the situation.

VIII. MONITORING THE IMPLEMENTATION OF THE SCHEME

The implementation of the scheme of decentralization outlined above needs to be nurtured carefully, which requires close monitoring. Such monitoring has to be dispassionate and objective, which can be only done by an independent body, bearing the interest of the state in mind. We are of the view that monitoring of the implementation of the scheme of decentralization should be entrusted to the Poverty Eradication Mission, set up by the Government of Andhra Pradesh to assist the CM in policy making, a task which falls within the Terms of Reference of the Mission. Since the system of planning and implementation of development programmes outlined above partakes the nature of reforming development governance, the Poverty Eradication Mission would make periodic reviews to a Cabinet Sub-committee which may be constituted for monitoring economic reforms and poverty reduction. The Poverty Eradication Mission could also concurrently monitor the impact of reform on poverty reduction and social development.

IX. SUMMARY OF RECOMMENDATIONS

In summary, we, therefore, make the following recommendations:

1. The District Planning Committee as enjoined in Article 243ZD of the Constitution may be constituted with powers to prepare a bottom up District Plan.
2. That Mandal Level and Gram Panchayat Level Planning Committees be concurrently established. The PRIs together with the SHGs will form *the first tier of planning for development.*
3. That a symbiotic relationship be worked out between the SHGs and the PRIs by statutorily making the members of the self-help groups members of the Standing Committees of the PRIs at all the tiers.
4. That a system of planning using participatory techniques and methods, starting from the village level upwards be established for convergence of programmes at the planning stage.
5. That functions, functionaries and finances in respect of nineteen subjects more fully described in Annexure hereto, be transferred through framing of Rules under the Andhra Pradesh Panchayati Raj Act 1994 to be subsequently enacted as Schedules to the said Act. And limits of authority of development administrators, elected representatives to the legislatures and the PRIs are notified. These measures will be informed by the principle of subsidiarity to ensure convergence of programmes at the implementation stage.

It is underscored here that it may be necessary to considerably strengthen the capability and capacity of the SHGs and the PRIs for the scheme of convergence outlined here to succeed.

References

Chattopadhyay, Srikumar; Krishna Kumar, P. and Rajalakshmi, K. (1999): *Panchayat Resource Mapping to Panchayat-Level Planning in Kerala: An Analytical Study* (Thiruvananthapuram: Centre for Development Studies), Discussion Paper No. 14.

Etherington, David and Paddon, Michael (1991): "The Free Local Government Initiative in Denmark—Modernization, Innovation or Control", in *Local Government Studies,* Vol. 17, No. 4, pp. 6-13.

Gaiha, Raghav (1997): *Decentralization: The Indian Experience* (Rome: Food and Agriculture Organization of the United Nations).

Government of Karnataka (1997): *Panchayati Raj in Karnataka* (Bangalore: Department of Rural Development & Panchayati Raj).

Government of India : Report of the Task Force on Devolution of Powers and Functions upon PRIs, 2001 (New Delhi : Ministry of Rural Development).

Harris, John (2000): "Renewing Development and Deepening Democracy" in *Frontline,* September 1st, 2001, pp. 75-76.

Misra, Surya Kanta and Sen, Ardhendu (1985): *Village Based District Planning Process: An Outline of Methodology* (Midnapore: District Planning Committee).

Mukherjee, Amitava (1995): *Participatory Rural Appraisal and Rural Development Planning* (New Delhi: Vikas).

Mukherjee, Neela (2001): *Participatory Learning and Action, with 100 Field Methods* (New Delhi: Concept Publishing Company).

Sanantonio, Enzo (1987): "Italy" in Page, Edward C. *et al.* (eds.): *Central and Local Government Relations: A Comparative Analysis of West European Unitary States* (London: Sage Publications).

Schmidt, V. A. (1990): *Democratizing France: The Political and Administrative History of Decentralization* (Cambridge: Cambridge University Press).

Isaac Thomas, T. M. *et al.* (2000): *Local Democracy and Development: People's Campaign for Decentralized Planning in Kerala* (New Delhi: Left Word Books).

APPENDIX A

CRITICAL ROLES OF THE MANDAL PARISHADS

(a) The objectives and aspirations of the Village Plans and Gram Panchayat Plans are fully included in the Mandal Level Plans so that the need will and aspirations of the people are correctly articulated in the Mandal Level Plans.

(b) The Mandal Praja Parishads will provide vertical integration between Village Plans, Gram Panchayats and the District Plans in developing and framing plans.

(c) A systematic collection and collation of plans in respect of all the Gram Panchayats within the territorial jurisdiction of the Mandal.

(d) The Mandal Panchayat will then separate plans, schemes or programmes that involve more than one Gram Panchayat from plans, schemes or programmes, which can be implemented in individual Gram Panchayats. The former should be examined and included in the Mandal Panchayat Plan and the latter should be kept as Gram Panchayat Level Plans.

(e) The Mandal Praja Parishads will then prepare a plan in respect of those sectors, which are to be implemented at the Mandal Panchayat level on their own motion or upon the delegated authority to do so by the state government. The Mandal Praja Parishads will include in such a Plan the plans, schemes and programmes, which the Gram Panchayat plans have generated for the Mandal Praja Parishads as stated in (iv) above.

(f) Those plans, schemes or programmes, which have been prepared for the Mandal Panchayat as a whole but which cannot be taken up for implementation at the Mandal Panchayat level as they involve more than one Mandal Praja Parishads, must be identified. These must be mentioned in the Mandal Panchayat Plan as the schemes to be included while preparing the Mandal level Plans.

(g) The Mandal Parishads would identify those schemes, programmes and projects which are made by the respective Mandals but which cannot be planned and implemented at Mandal level. These would be segregated in the Mandal Plans as "District Sector Plan" and recommended for inclusion within the purview of the district plan.

7

Panchayats and Democracy[1]

Elites versus Dalits

D. Bandyopadhyay

In the lexicon of social science in India, the word *'dalit'* has acquired a specific connotation mainly relating to the caste origin of a group of people who are clubbed under this term. In this Chapter, I am using the word in a much broader sense, which would encompass all people who are exploited, oppressed or suppressed because of social, religious, economic or political reasons, irrespective of their caste or ethnic origin. Under this definition, a dispossessed or exploited Brahmin or a Rajput would be a *dalit*, while the creamy layer of scheduled castes and scheduled tribes would be excluded. I know, some Indian sociologists would strongly contest this position. Without engaging in a controversy with the *'pandits'*, I would maintain this stance in expounding the dynamics of political discourse in rural India after the introduction of the constitutionally mandated third tier of governance at the district level and below, following the 73rd Constitution Amendment Act. It is recognized that *'dalit'*, whether under the new or the old connotation, is not a homogeneous aggregation of people. *Dalits* have some commonality in abstraction. But, in reality, this is as much a fractured group as any other section of the society.

It is desirable to discuss why, almost 40 years after the introduction of the Constitution, there was a renewal of interest

1. Originally published in Man and Development, Chandigarh.

in the panchayat system, during the closing years of the prime ministership of late Rajiv Gandhi.

The founding fathers of the Constitution did not discuss about Panchayats while drafting the Constitution. They totally ignored the issue. Dr. B. R. Ambedkar, the main draftsman of the document, had 'expressed himself against the system of village Panchayats'. Characterizing the village as 'a sink of localism' and 'a den of narrow-mindedness', he had observed, "I am glad that the Constitution has discarded the village and adopted the individual as a unit".

When Gandhiji came to know that the final draft of the Constitution did not contain anything on Panchayats, he felt both disturbed and depressed. Presumably, noticing his distress, Shri K. Santanam moved an amendment on inserting the present Article 40 — 'Organisation of Village Panchayats' in Part IV of the Constitution — Directive Principles of State Policy. Without any debate, almost absent-mindedly, the amendment was accepted. It was, perhaps, a sop to an old man's predeliction.

There is no point in recording the well-known history of Panchayats in post-independent India. The post-Balwantrai Mehta - Mark I Panchayats of Maharashtra and Gujarat were hailed as models. But, soon, the political elites, often belonging to the same ruling party, started decimating them, to keep the power unto themselves. An extra-constitutional power centre was created in the shape of 'Guardian' minister of the district to overshadow the chairperson of the Zila Parishad. The post-Ashok Mehta Committee - Mark II Panchayats of West Bengal, Andhra Pradesh, Karnataka and Kerala were well spoken of for devolution of power and authority and regularity of election processes. But, in the southern states, the Mark-II Panchayats met the same fate as the first generation Panchayats earlier, once the political parties, which had resurrected these, lost power. In West Bengal, the Panchayat system survived because the Left Front and the Panchayats have been supporting each other in retaining power through the election process.

Against this thumb-nail historical sketch of Panchayats in India, it is a bit of a riddle why and how Rajiv Gandhi— a totally apolitical person to begin with—did realize, appreciate and with single-minded devotion and determination activate and ancient and currently defunct system of governance at the local level—the Panchayat.

In post-independence Union, Panchayats were initially looked upon as an add-on accessory for enhancing the efficacy of the existing district administrative machinery. With the waning of popular support for the community development programme in the second phase, a search was initiated to find ways and means for enhancing power participation. Balwantrai Mehta's answer was Panchayats, which were designated to perform development functions along with the existing development administration—BDO, VLW, *et al.* Then it went into almost disuse. The Gandhian Janata Government in 1977, which introduced the programme of 'antyodya' found that the existing district administrative machinery was unable to reach the 'last' person. Another quest began. Ashok Mehta's two-tier Panchayat was supposed to be the answer. It was again the 'development only' Panchayats supplementing basically the administrative efforts. Rajiv Gandhi's probe too started for the same purpose.

Search for Efficient Delivery System

His first significant statement on Panchayats was made in his inaugural address to the 13th All India Panchayat Parishad's meeting in September 1986, almost two years after he became Prime Minister. Here one finds the same search for an efficient delivery system which prompted the community development authorities to appoint the Balwantrai Mehta Committee in the late fifties. He said: "If we continue to devise schemes from able, large sections of the population will be left high and dry, and flow of benefits from development will pass over their heads like water on a duck's back, for it is not possible for the government agencies to reach each and every individual and to guide him and tell him to do this or that".

Having been in office for two years and having gone round the country fairly widely, he received complaints about leakage and misuse of resources of the massive rural development programmes. He was worried and he started looking for an alternative system. Even so, having seen the limitation of the existing development organisation, he was still not prepared to take any radical stance. All that he was willing to think was that the outreach of government agencies being limited, the panchayat had to be brought in as a supplementary or balancing measure to the existing structure. The idea was quite far from the concept of democracy at the doorstep, which he stridently advocated later.

His continuous tour of rural India and his direct talks and contact with numerous rural people, ethnic and minority groups, made him feel that there was something essential missing in the vast administrative apparatus at the district level and below. That missing link, he realized, was responsiveness. And this was due to the absence of accountability of the bureaucracy to the people it was to serve. He found that while the civil services had the finest brains and the best administrative ability in the country, 'the experience of the vast majority of our people at the grassroots have been that, at the interface between the people and the administration, the administration is unresponsive, inefficient, unsympathetic, often callous, sometimes even cruel to those whom they are meant to serve'. There had never been a more severe indictment of the district administration from a Prime Minister than this.

He was intrigued. He was determined to find out both the reason and the solution. He undertook a massive exercise of meeting all the District Magistrates and Collectors of India in five workshops on 'Responsive Administration'. He started rather hesitantly and tentatively. But all his hesitation, apprehension and doubt disappeared when he addressed the last workshop at Coimbatore in June 1988. There was no doubt or ambiguity in his statement. He admitted that when he began the series of workshops of 'Responsive Administration' his attention was primarily focused on the nitty-gritty of problems at the interface between the district administration and the people which the administration was designed to serve. But soon it became clear that the underlying problem was not so much a matter of simplifying procedures or establishing grievance redressal machinery but fundamentally of a systemic nature. It quickly becomes apparent that if our district administration is not sufficiently responsive, the basic reason is that it is not sufficiently representative'.

For a Sea Change in the Mindset

It was no longer a matter of tinkering with the existing system. It was no longer an issue of a balancing or a supplementary effort. It was a question of a basic change in the administrative system at the district level and below, from a non-representative autocratic and bureaucratic administration to a representative and responsive elected system of governance. A sea change in the mindset.

Thus, in a way, the search for an alternative supplementary system resulted in almost supplanting the apparatus. While commending the new proposal of a representative type of district administration to the Conference of Chief Ministers Rajiv Gandhi said, "Never before has a government at the highest level taken so carefully into account the views of so many tens of thousands of people at every level, about democracy and development at the grassroots. The proposals we place before you are not really our proposals. They are the proposals of the people of India".

These are all recorded and manifested reasons. They are genuine. But, behind the entire programme there were other factors which one should not ignore. The seventies and the eighties were turbulent decades for the Indian Republic. There was militant movement in different parts of the country. The Republic was clearly under severe stress, not only at its periphery but also in its heartland. The Gorkhaland agitation, with its high level of militancy, almost threatened to lead to a third partition of West Bengal. There was the Jharkhand movement in Central India. Obviously, there were groups—ethnic, religious, linguistic—who felt that they were not part of the mainstream of India. To assert their identity, to uphold their specificity, to claim their uniqueness, they all clamoured for state power to shape their own destinies in their own way. The repressive machinery of the state could not satisfactorily cope with them. These groups had to be co-opted. And that could be through power sharing. The constitutionally mandated Panchayats, defined as institutions of self-government, could be the ideal mechanism for bringing together the disintegrating fractions of the society. And looking back, it did not succeed substantially. The third factor was of short-term consequence. Rajiv Gandhi, during his tenure of prime ministership, faced a tremendous demand for greater powers for the states. The so-called 'Opposition' Chief Ministers, which included such stalwarts as Jyoti Basu, N.T. Rama Rao, Ramakrishna Hegde *et al.*, mounted a sustained campaign. The Sarkaria Commission gave its report in 1983. Many Chief Ministers were up against the Central Government for the 'misuse' of Article 356. They clamoured for more fiscal powers: Often, rattled by such moves, some counsel was given why not create separate foci of power within the states through the constitutionally created Panchayats, which would in their turn pose similar problems for the Chief Ministers for sharing state power? One can say that was the flip side of an otherwise genuine exercise for seeking an alternative to the existing bureaucratic district administration and for mainstreaming the alienated groups in the society.

Almost Non-accountable Bureaucratic Administration

In order to appreciate what changes the 73rd Constitution Amendment Act brought about in the district administration, it would be desirable to have a quick look at the system of governance in the country prior to this Amendment. We had, and still have, a very vibrant and vigorous democracy functioning at the Central and State levels, invigorated by regular and even frequent general elections. But prior to the 73rd Amendment, there was an almost non-accountable bureaucratic administration below the state level. Whether revenue or health or police or any development administration, except the constructive accountability of the minister to the legislature, the officers were not accountable to those over whom they exercised power and authority. Exercise of power was downwards and the nominal accountability upwards. And there was an in-built institutional bias to protect the subordinates against any ordinary complaints. Any negligence or abuse of power by a subordinate reflected badly on the supervisory officer, who failed to prevent it. Hence, the best policy was to cover up and avoid any further botheration and hassle.

The pictograph crudely represents the situation that obtained before the constitutional amendment. In his dissenting note to the Ashok Mehta Committee Report, E.M.S. Namboodiripad graphically described the situation. He stated:

Democracy at the Central and State levels, but bureaucracy at all lower levels—that is the essence of Indian polity as spelt out in the Constitution.

I cannot think of the Panchayati Raj Institutions as anything other than the integral parts of the country's administration, with no difference between what are called the 'development' and 'regulatory' functions ... I am afraid the ghost of the earlier idea that Panchayati Raj Institutions should be completely divorced from all regulatory functions and made to confine themselves only to the developmental functions is haunting my colleagues.

E.M.S. conceived of Panchayats as institutions supplanting the non-representative steel frame at the district level and below. In 1978, he was far ahead of his time but he showed the right direction.

One might argue that MLAs and MPs are there to look after the interests of the electorate, even without a third tier of representative system of governance at the district level. One has to be aware of the physical and other limitations from which they suffer. An MP is supposed to represent one million electors. In fact, today he might be representing around 1.5 million electors. Population figures could be much higher. An MLA is supposed to represent 100,000 electors. But he actually represents many more, as the constituencies have been demarcated on the basis of population figures of the 1971

PYRAMID OF POWER
(Prior to 73rd Constitution Amendment)

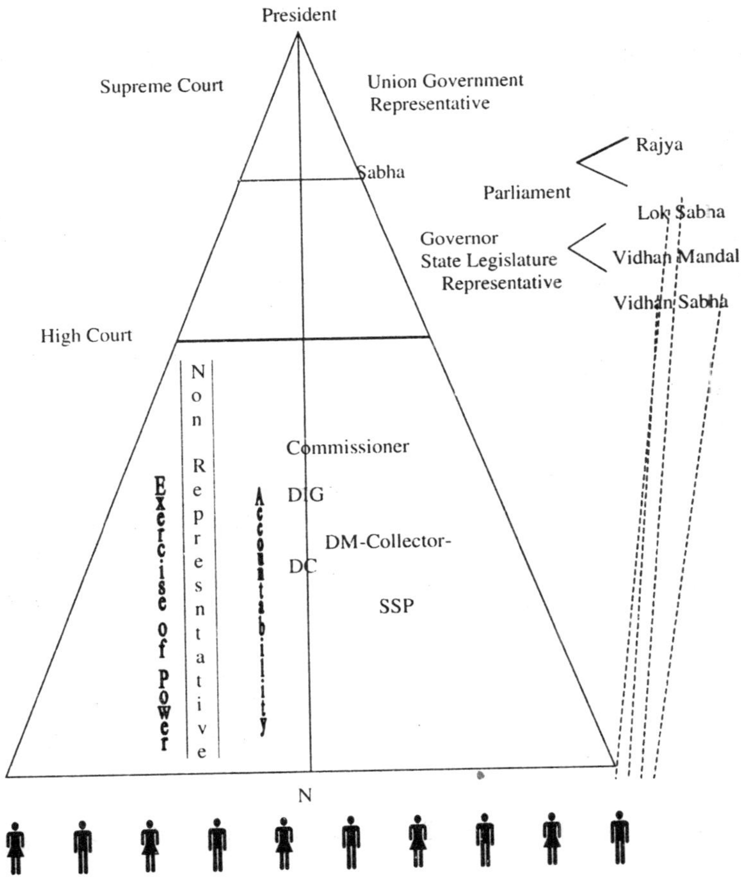

Electors - People of India

Census. Even the best of MPs and MLAs cannot have direct physical access to each one of their electors. The Central and State Governments are too far removed from the masses. The bureaucratic district administration, by its very nature, would get isolated from the people; 'thus dulling its sensitivity to the needs of the people'. Rajiv Gandhi described the situation vividly in a succinct manner. He stated :

The present chasm between a few elected representatives like MPs and MLAs and the bureaucratic district administration and the vast masses was conveniently filled up by power brokers, the middle men, the vested interests. The power brokers have established their vice-like grip only because democracy has not functioned at the grassroots. Once the people have their own elected representatives from electorates as small as a hundred to five hundred persons, the source of power will lie only as far away as the Panchayat Ghar, not some distant state capital or even more distant capital of the country.

Rajiv Gandhi envisaged Panchayats as governments unto themselves for the limited powers vested in them. Panchayats would no longer be the unpaid elected extension agencies of the development administration.

I have referred to Rajiv Gandhi rather extensively only to highlight the point that, but for his initiative and stubborn prodding, the 64th Amendment Bill could not have been introduced. Otherwise, the elite political establishment would have scuttled the move for empowering the powerless through Panchayats, as they had successfully sidetracked the issue for the last 40 years in spite of Article 40 in the Constitution. One could only speculate on the motive of Rajiv Gandhi. It could be that, being a novice in the political establishment, he was quite wary of the existing power centres. Hence, through creating counterpoints, he wanted to secure a strong political base. Though he was politically strongly opposed to the Left Front Government of West Bengal, he appreciated its ability of rooting itself strongly in the rural areas through Panchayats and a modicum of land reforms. That might have given him the idea that if he could have elected foci of power below the state level, it would help him cut to size the powers of the states while enhancing his influence all over the country. It could also have been his dissatisfaction with the inefficient delivery system of the existing district apparatus that spurred him to seek a radical change. It might also have been a patrician's commiseration with the plebians. Be that as it may, there is no denying that Rajiv Gandhi set in motion a process of changing the architecture of Indian polity, which found expression in the 73rd Constitution Amendment Act. It introduced the third tier of representative governance at the district level and below.

Panchayats are Institutions of Self-government

For subsequent discussion, it would be desirable to state briefly the salient features of Part IX of the Constitution (The Panchayats). In the first place, 'Panchayat means an institution (by whatever name called) of self-government constituted under Article 243-B for rural areas'. This definition has been fortified by Article 243-G which states, 'Subject to the provisions of the Constitution, the Legislature of a State may by law, endow the Panchayats with such powers and authority as may be necessary to enable them to function as institutions of self-government'. Thus, Panchayats are as much institutions of self-government as the State or the Central Government. Of course, they do not have legislative or judicial powers to qualify as governments *per se*, but as institutions of self-government their autonomy is guaranteed by the Constitution.

There are two aspects of the powers of the Panchayats : original powers and functions and delegated powers and functions. The original power and function of a Panchayat at each tier is

'243-G ......

(a) the preparation of plans for economic development and social justice.'

The delegated powers and functions relate to 'the implementation of schemes for economic development and social justice as may be entrusted to them including those in relation to the matters listed in the Eleventh Schedule'.

The salient features are the constitution of a State Finance Commission for fair sharing of resources and a State Election Commission for ensuring regularity and fairness of elections and reservation of (not less than one-third) seats and positions for women and scheduled castes and scheduled tribes and OBCs in proportion to their population. All these features clearly indicate the creation of a third tier of representative governance at the district level and below.

Now let us revert to the original functions of Panchayats. The Planning Commission of India is not a constitutional entity. It is not even a statutory body. In contrast, Part IX of the Constitution mandates Panchayats to prepare plans for economic development and social justice. Perhaps, with the unsavoury experience of economic planning by the Planning Commission, which accelerated the rate of growth of the gross domestic product and simultaneously accentuated income and asset differentiation among the different segments of the society, the Parliament directed that the plans for economic development prepared by the Panchayats should simultaneously ensure social justice. The two clauses have to be read conjunctively. Panchayats cannot prepare economic plans which do not ensure social justice. A tall order, but that is what it is. The intention clearly is to promote social justice. The masses, particularly the deprived masses, should play an active, nay, proactive role in the preparation of the plan, at least at the lowest tier — the Gram Panchayat. Only the victims of social injustice could, through their direct participation in the planning process, promote social justice. This feature clearly makes Panchayats democracy for the *dalits*.

The elite did not take long to strike back. It took its revenge through the 74th Amendment which followed the 73rd. Article 243-ZD directs the creation of a District Planning Committee (DPC) at the district level 'to consolidate the plans prepared by the Panchayats and municipalities in the district and to prepare a draft Development Plan for the district as a whole'. The draft Plan, so prepared and recommended by the DPC, would be forwarded to the State Government.

Under 243-G, Panchayats prepare plans for economic development. Since there is no qualification, their plans should be treated as final. Now, at the district level, when the same plans are consolidated, they become draft plans. Here is the first contradiction. The second contradiction is that there is nothing in the Constitution to indicate how much of these district plans would be integrated in the state plan. Theoretically, state plans could be prepared quite independently of the district draft plans, containing none of their programmes.

In that event, such a mammoth exercise, starting from the village (even wards) upwards would become meaningless. It would be a mockery of the planning process from below, (so assiduously crafted in these amendments) as contra-distinguished from planning from the top, to which the country has been accustomed for the last four decades and a half.

A Rational and Harmonious Interpretation

In the absence of a judicial determination or a further amendment to the Constitution, a rational and harmonious interpretation would be that, at each tier of the Panchayats, plans for economic development and social justice prepared by it would be implemented by it within its territorial jurisdiction with its own resources and technical competence. Those elements of the plan, which they are unable to implement, either because of their possible impact outside their territorial jurisdiction, or because of resource constraints, or lack of expertise, would be forwarded to the next higher level. Thus, at the district level, the draft plan would consist of those residuary elements, which the Zila Parishads and the municipalities would not be able to implement because of any one or more of the reasons mentioned above. To this extent the district plan would assume a tentative character and, therefore could be designated a 'draft plan'. According to this interpretation, the tentative nature of the district plan, consisting of the residuary elements, which would be forwarded to the state government, cannot take away or in any way reduce or diminish the substantive power of the preparation of plans for economic development and social justice and their effective implementation at each tier of the Panchayats.

Only one state government in India, i.e. Kerala has seriously implemented this provision under Article 243-G through its programme of people's participation in the preparation of the Ninth Plan. Many of the state governments have refused even to pay lip service to this interpretation and implement sectoral plans of various departments through their own bureaucracy, using the Panchayat as mere extension agencies as and when necessary. The elite did not concede even an iota of ground on this issue.

As mentioned earlier, Panchayats are institutions of self-government. A basic feature of any such institution is autonomy — autonomy in matters of resources, autonomy in decision-making in respect of powers and functions assigned and autonomy in implementing decisions through its own functionaries. One can say that there is a 3-F formula— Functions, Finance, Functionary. With the assignment of functions by law, corresponding finances of the state budget have to be given to Panchayats, along with such functionaries as were already engaged in these activities under the state government. Without control over these 3Fs, Panchayats would be elected subordinate officers under the state government. The Constitution provides some safeguards to prevent such contingencies.

States Empower Themselves

To prevent the executive branch of the state government from playing ducks and drakes with the powers and functions of Panchayats, Article 243-G clearly lays down that only the legislature of a state will endow Panchayats with such powers and authority as to enable them to function as institutions of self-government. Many state governments have neatly bypassed the spirit, and often the letter, of this Article by enacting laws empowering themselves to assign or withdraw any power and function to and from Panchayats.

Without citing many examples I shall just quote a provision from the West Bengal Panchayats (Amendment) Act 1994 in respect of this issue. It states :

> Without prejudice to the generality of the provision contained in Section 207 or elsewhere, the State may, by order published in the official gazette, transfer under such terms and conditions as may be specified in the order, to a Panchayat, such powers, functions and duties as are exercised, performed and discharged by the State Government under any law by the State legislature or otherwise under the

> executive power of the State in relation to any or all the following matters.

A plain reading of this convoluted section is that the executive branch of the government can give to or take away any powers, functions and duties from Panchayats at any time at its sweet will, thus, bringing in arbitrariness in the entire transaction which Article 243-G specifically wanted to avoid. But who cares?

In Madhya Pradesh, the government transferred 22 departments to Panchayats. Later on, it withdrew four or five departments under pressure from the elite political establishment. It has at least kept some 17 or 18 departments with Panchayats. Similar is the case with many other state governments. Kerala has carried out a systematic study by the Sen Committee and is trying to implement its recommendations. Some time ago, MLAs in Karnataka gave an ultimatum to the Chief Minister that unless they were made chairpersons of the site-and-house distribution committees of taluka Panchayats, there would be a revolt. The government buckled under the pressure and yielded. A concession once given is difficult to withdraw. Hence, the aberration is most likely to continue in spite of changes in government. If external elements rule the roost, where is the autonomy? And what happens to the legally mandated concept of 'institution of self-government'?

By and large, in many states, Panchayats are being treated as extension agencies of the executive line departments rather than as institutions of self-government. Functions and powers are not being devolved to them. Instead, what is being done is the delegation of functions with the right retained by the state government to take away, abridge, mutilate or alter such arrangements through executive order without the consent of the legislature. Continuation of such agencies as DRDA, FFDA and the like, which are independent of the Zila Parishad, is anathema to the concept of democracy. But, instead of abolishing such bodies and merging them with the Zila Parishads, both the Government of India and the State

Governments are not merely continuing with them but are adding to the list, circumscribing the powers, authority and prestige of Panchayats. Multilateral funding bodies are very fond of creating a one line administration for each one of their funded programmes, with *ad hoc* committees at the state headquarters and the district level with bureaucrats and technocrats together with a sprinkling of some favoured NGO representation, as members for channelling funds, implementing projects and monitoring their progress. They insist and the state governments, eager to get some funds, easily succumb, creating more problems for the Panchayats.

Unwilling to Lose Control

Ideally, all functionaries at different levels should be placed with the appropriate tier of the Panchayat along with the devolution of functions. This is not being done in most of the states. In Gram Panchayat area, there are at least a couple of dozens of government functionaries from different departments, operating independently under their own department bosses. If all of them had been placed under the control of the Panchayats, services would have improved significantly. In a few states, where primary schools and lower-level health functionaries have been placed under Panchayats, the attendance of teachers has improved, enrollment of students increased and dropout rates have decreased. Visits of health workers have become regular. But neither were the staff willing to be accountable to the Panchayats, nor the departmental bosses, often including ministers, to lose 'control' and 'command' over them, resulting in a chaotic situation at the ground level. Often, there is a subtle but concerted move to denigrate the Panchayats before their own constituencies. Rules about public works in most states are antiquated, out of date and dysfunctional. In this context, an entity called Junior Engineer becomes the real boss. No project can be undertaken without his sanction. No project can be completed without his completion certificate. The devious market mechanism often operates, threatening both the quality and quantity of public works. Unlike government departments, where the decision-makers are invisible to the public, elected Panchayat functionaries work in the full glare of public visibility. Thus, manipulations by the Junior Engineer are considered to be by the elected functionary, resulting in the corrosion of his popular base. This avoidable and unnecessary interference by the bureaucracy could be easily set right by allowing authorized private engineering consultancy firms to fulfil the same task on payment of fees. Works would be completed quicker, cheaper and with greater public satisfaction. But the vested interests in the line departments would not allow this, as the government at the higher level does not have the will to do so. This is just an example. Such accusations were made openly and publicly at each one of the 45 sub-regional workshops of elected Panchayat functionaries held all over the country by the Rajiv Gandhi Foundation.

Further, in the name of control and supervision, the bureaucracy has been given overriding powers over elected Panchayats in every state legislation. Such laws permit the higher echelons of the bureaucracy to suspend and supersede Panchayats. In a couple of states, the Act had given the Chief Executive Officer of the Zila Parishad the authority to refuse to implement any of its resolutions, if considered by him not to be in the public interest. An absurd proposition. But there it was. One is tempted to ask, how would a Chief Minister of a state relish the idea of his Chief Secretary being given the power to rescind or renege the decision of the State Cabinet if considered by him not to be in the public interest? It makes a mockery of the concept of self-government.

Peer Group Accountability Required

What is necessary and desirable is that elected Panchayats should not be subordinate to government officials. Elected representatives should have the right to exercise superintendence and control over government officials to be placed under the Panchayats along with devolution of functions. The power of dissolution, as well as of accountability of lower-level Panchayat units must rest with the next higher-level of Panchayats and not with government officials, so that peer group accountability is established.

Finances of panchayats, one of the three pillars of their autonomy (the other two being proper devolution of functions and control and superintendence over functionaries), is a fairly technical subject. I do not wish to enter into a technical discussion on it here. I would like to recount briefly some salient points : just to emphasize the issue, that a lot more requires to be done by the state governments in this regard if they are serious about making governance at the doorstep function better.

Article 243-I provides for the constitution of a State Finance Commission (SFC) by each state to review the financial position of Panchayats and make recommendations, which the Governor would place before the legislature, with an explanatory memorandum as to the action taken thereon. Obviously, the intention of the Constitution is to ensure financial independence of Panchayats and to immune them from arbitrary and *ad hoc* decisions of the state government regarding flow of funds to Panchayats. The State Finance Commissions have to decide on the assignment of taxes, duties, fees and levies of Panchayats. Secondly, they have to determine which of the state-level taxes have to be shared between the state and the Panchayats. Thirdly, they have to settle what should be the grant-in-aid policy towards Panchayats. There is an omnibus clause which enjoins upon the SFCs to decide measures necessary to augment the resources of Panchayats. Over a period of time, conventionally, four or five taxes have come to be devolved to Panchayats. The SFCs have preferred to leave the tax domain of Panchayats largely unchanged. Three distinct features, however, emerge out of the various SFC reports.

- Autonomy in determining the tax base, such as, who would decide on exemption — who would be or would not be taxed — rests with the state government. There is no reference in any SFC report that the power to fix tax and to decide the tax base should be devolved to Panchayats.

- SFCs have allowed even entertainment and professional taxes to be within the state's domain, with a provision that proceeds of the entertainment tax should be distributed among the local bodies. But the power to collect it continues to rest with the state government.
- Only a couple of SFCs have recommended the need to review the manner in which these taxes are levied, assessed and valued. The Kerala SFC, for instance, has suggested that the entire system of property tax assessment should be changed from annual rate valuation to site valuation.

Sharing certain state-level taxes is standard practice, universally. In India, traditionally, the motor vehicles tax and the stamp duty—both state-level taxes—have been shared by local bodies in some proportion. Though most of the SFCs have been maintaining the *status quo*, in some reports two or three significant changes have been proposed. In the first place, they have suggested replacement of a fixed amount by a percentage of the total revenue collected on these heads. Secondly, instead of sharing individual taxes there should be a notional sharing of taxes, that is, out of the total tax receipts of the state government, 'X' percentage is to be assigned to Panchayats and 'Y' percentage to municipalities. This is in tune with the recommendations of the National Development Council, which has, *inter alia* proposed that 29 per cent of the total tax receipts of the Central Government should be assigned to State Governments. But here again one finds wide variations from state to state in the proportion of taxes to be shared.

The grant-in-aid system had always been very *ad hoc* in our country. As a result, there had been continuous unpredictability about the actual flow of funds to Panchayats, both in terms of the amount and timing. In some states, the number of grants goes up from 64, under different heads. That apart, many grants are tied to the performance of specific state functions. One would have expected the SFCs to recommend one single general-purpose grant, which could be used by the

Panchayats in accordance with local development priorities. But nothing of the sort has been done. Except in the case of a few SFCs, which have advocated a reduction in the number of heads under which grants are given, the recommendations give a confused picture.

The reports of the SFCs are quite inadequate and often dismal with regard to the aspect of general augmentation of resources of Panchayats. Many SFCs have suggested privatization of some the municipal services such as solid waste disposal, drainage, maintenance of roads, etc. Most of them seem to have been affected by the general environment of liberalization, deregulation and privatization. Proposals are not all well thought out. They look more like slogan-mongering rather than hard fiscal propositions. In defiance of the SFCs, one can say that all of them had to explore uncharted territory, without any precedent. There was no guideline. And most of them seemed to have been more concerned with the resources crunch, from which almost all the states were suffering. Moreover, improvement of the finances of Panchayats is a long drawn-out process. Hence, it cannot be solved by one round of recommendations of SFCs.

SFC Recommendations Not Implemented

Much more ominous than the inability of the SFCs to do something substantial for Panchayats is the total lack of seriousness with which the state governments have dealt with the SFCs and their recommendations of the SFCs fully. Even those which accepted them fully did hardly anything to implement them. The SFCs were at a great disadvantage as they were never told how many items of the Eleventh Schedule would be devolved to Panchayats and in what manner. Without any knowledge of the volume of business the Panchayats would have to handle and the number of state functionaries to be deployed under the control of the Panchayats to discharge these functions, the SFCs could hardly do anything but tinker with the existing arrangements. Of course, the SFCs could have asked for a bulk untied grant, to enable Panchayats discharge their mandatory functions of preparations of plans for economic development and social justice. But this they have not done. Perhaps in course of time, a sort of Gadgil formula would be evolved for allocation of plan funds between states and Zila Parishads. But for that one has to wait and see.

Article 280(3) (bb) has mandated the Central Finance Commission to recommend 'the measures needed to augment the Consolidated Fund of a State to supplement the resources of the Panchayats in the state on the basis of the recommendations of the Finance Commission of the State'. The Tenth Finance Commission did not have the benefit of the recommendations of any SFC. Even so, they recommended some *ad hoc* transfer. It is now for the Eleventh Finance Commission to lay down sound principles and suggest measures to put the Panchayat finances on a strong footing. Unless something radical is done, the continued dependence of Panchayats on state resources would never allow them to be autonomous.

Those who have had the privilege of exchanging views with the elected members and functionaries extensively have found that they often felt that they were being stymied, obstructed, hindered and prevented by the bureaucracy and MLAs/MPs from discharging their constitutional roles. They were not being taken seriously. They were not being given powers, functions, finances and functionaries to make the Panchayats effective institutions of self-government as directed by the Constitution. There were frequent wilful attempts to make them appear as a bunch of ineffective and incompetent women and men incapable of fulfilling the desires and aspirations of their constituents.

Bureaucrats and Ministers Create Road-blocks

The bureaucracy reacted to the post-amendment situation in two ways. At the Heads-of-Department level, they looked at the devolution of powers, functions and finances to Panchayats as a direct threat to their patronage-and-influence-peddling capability. Departmental Ministers (across party lines), also under the same threat perception, very often sided with the bureaucracy. Hence, road-blocks were skilfully put up to prevent flow of funds and functions from state headquarters to Panchayats. At the district level and below, the bureaucracy, accustomed to lord over the administration, openly resented the intrusion by Panchayats into their close preserve. They felt uncomfortable, uneasy and uncertain, because of their being held accountable for their actions and inactions, by the elected Panchayat functionaries and members. The reversal of the role from 'overloading' to being 'lorded over' was something many in the bureaucracy found unacceptable. 'The bureaucracy in general would prefer the *status quo* to be frozen in perpetuity' (Meenakshisundaram, S.S., 1995).

In a two-tier system of representative government, that we had till the 73rd Amendment came into existence, MPs, and more so, MLAs had acquired a great deal of influence and even executive powers, primarily because of the absence of any representative system of governance at the district level and below. Distribution of patronage and benefits being essential ingredients of management of constituencies, many MLAs and MPs felt threatened by the possible loss of these privileges with the advent of Panchayat institutions of self-government. This apprehension created two situations. In the first place, these people's representatives, numbering less than 5,000 (MPs and MLAs all over India), went on entrenching themselves more firmly with more powers, perks and privileges. For instance, an MP's Local Area Development Fund of one crore rupees became two crore rupees overnight, with similar funds for MLAs in some states being doubled. Secondly, the state legislative assemblies have been failing (barring a few exceptions) in fulfilling the constitutional obligation to make Panchayats, institutions of self-government, by not devolving powers and functions (George Mathew, 1999).

This sordid state of affairs has been well described by the veteran parliamentarian, C. Subramaniam. Deploring the sad current situation he observed, 'When important legislation comes up for discussion, empty benches and lack of quorum often force adjournments. Apathy on the part of members also facilitates major legislation entering statute books without adequate consideration of related issues and concerns. These constitute dereliction of duty on the part of the members of Parliament'. He described the MP's Local Area Development Fund as unethical and commented :

Such 'pork-barrel' funds have an inherent potential for misapplication and worse. This also involves members of legislatures taking on executive functions and infringes the constitutionally mandated separation of the executive and legislative branches of government ... If the members of Parliament appear to be obsessed with self-interest at the cost of national interest and if they are perceived by the public at large as enjoying privileges without shouldering corresponding new responsibilities, they will unwillingly become visible wrong role-models.

The fact is that the democracy of the elites is on the offensive against the democracy of the *dalits*. The elites are out to destroy democracy and/or make it non-functional. The democracy of the *dalits* is at a disadvantage. It is not the product of a mass movement. There was no ground swell forcing the political elites to concede saving grace is that *dalits* and women have tasted power, however small. In course of time, they might organize themselves and develop a massive force, under whose pressure the elite might concede all the powers indicated in the Constitution and more. The first quarter of the 21st century will witness this long struggle in which the *dalits* are most likely to win. Mahatmaji foresaw the situation long ago. On 7 July, 1947, he wrote in the *Harijan* :

> When Panchayat Raj is established, public opinion will do what violence can never do. The present power of the *zamindars*, the capitalists and the *rajas* can hold sway so long as the common people do not realize their own strength. If the people non-cooperate with the evil of *zamindary* or capitalism, it must die of inanition. In Panchayat Raj only the Panchayats will be obeyed and the Panchayats can only work through the law of their making.

Only history will tell who will win !

References

Bandyopadhyay, D. (1999): 'People's Participation in Planning – Kerala Experiment', *Economic and Political Weekly*, 27 September, 1999.

——— (1997): 'Voluntary Organisations and Panchayats', *Mainstream*, 29 March, 1997.

——— (1997): 'Panchayats and Personnel Policy', *Mainstream*, Annual Number.

——— (1994): *'Rajiv Gandhi and the Third Tier of Governance* (mimeo), November 1994.

Gandhi, M.K. (1947): *India of My Dreams*, Navajivan Publishing House.

Indira Gandhi National Open University, New Delhi,: *Evolution of Panchayati Raj and the Constitutional (73rd Amendment) Act, 1992*, Sponsored by the Ministry of Rural Areas and Employment, Government of India.

Mukarji, Nirmal and Bandyopadhyay D. (1993): *New Horizons for West Bengal's Panchayats : A Report for the Government of West Bengal*, October.

Mathur, Om Prakash (1999): *Decentralisation in India : A Report Card*, National Institute of Public Finance and Policy, March.

Publications Division, Government of India, *Rajiv Gandhi — Selected Speeches and Writings*, Volumes II, III, IV and V.

Rajiv Gandhi Foundation Task Force on Panchayati Raj: *Issues for Discussion in Sub-Regional Workshops - 1994-95 and Other Documents*, October 1994.

——— (1997): *Voices from Below*, November.

——— (1977): *Revitalisation of Panchayati Raj in India*.

——— (1998): *Proceedings of National Seminar on Panchayats, 22-23 December: 1997*, March.

——— (1999): *Road Block to the Institutions of Self-Government*, February.

——— (1999): *Dialogue on Panchayat : Summary Proceedings of Four Regional Tripartite Interface Interactive Workshops*, held between July 1998 and February 1999, April.

Regional Support Organisations (NCRSO) (1999): *Status of Finances of Panchayati Raj Institutions : An Overview*.

Society for Participatory Research in Asia (PRIA) and Network of Collaborating.

Index